Mother's Finest

Southern Cooking
Made Easy

Mother's Finest
Southern Cooking Made Easy

Published by Mother's Finest Catering
Copyright © 2002 by
Mother's Finest
1065 Veteran's Memorial Highway
Mableton, Georgia 30126
770-944-9277

This cookbook is a collection of favorite recipes, which are not necessarily original recipes.

ISBN: 0-9712749-0-8

Edited, Designed, and Manufactured by
Favorite Recipes® Press
an imprint of

FRP™

P.O. Box 305142
Nashville, Tennessee 37230
1-800-358-0560

Book Design: Steve Newman
Project Manager: Linda Bennie

Manufactured in the United States of America
First Printing: 2002   7,000 copies

Cover Art and Illustrations by Carol Baxter Kirby
Carol Baxter Kirby is a local American portrait painter and an artist of exceptional talent who exhibits the rare quality of capturing the inner depths of her subjects. Thanks, Carol, for taking time out of your busy schedule to illustrate this book.

Table of Contents

Dedication

To my daughter, Melinda, my sons and their spouses, Tony and Mary, James and Christy, and my grandchildren, Amy, Erin, and A. J., who allowed me to realize a dream and supported me with love; to my many friends who encouraged and helped during our early years in catering and in helping put this cookbook together; and to the many clients who have supported and continue to support us, I lovingly dedicate this book.

Introduction

This cookbook has been developed through the collaboration of the Ashcraft family and their friends. The Ashcrafts are the owners and operators of Mother's Finest Catering, a very successful business located in the suburbs of Atlanta, Georgia. The catering business actually began as a result of so many people asking Wilma Ashcraft, the matriarch of the family, for her homemade baked items and recipes.

Word of mouth from satisfied clients has made Mother's Finest one of the most successful catering businesses in the Atlanta area.

With the growing success of Mother's Finest Catering, the requests for copies of recipes also continues to grow, thus the inspiration for this book.

Recipes contained in this book are perfected old Southern traditional recipes and are very simple to reproduce using ingredients found in everyday kitchens. This book contains gourmet recipes, as well as ideas and tips to enable the most inexperienced cook to cook like an expert.

This is a must-have cookbook even if you have hundreds of other cookbooks.

Life's Recipe

1 cup of good thoughts
1 cup of kind deeds
1 cup of consideration for others
2 cups of sacrifice for others
3 cups of forgiveness
2 cups of well-beaten faults

Mix thoroughly and add tears of joy and sorrow and sympathy for others. Flavor with little gifts of love. Fold in 4 cups of prayer and faith to lighten other ingredients and raise the texture to great heights of Christian living. After pouring all this into your daily life, bake well with the heat of human kindness. Serve with a smile.

Appetizers
&
Beverages

rtichoke Dip

1 large can water-pack artichoke hearts,
   drained

2 cups mayonnaise
1¹/2 cups grated Parmesan cheese

Cut the artichokes into bite-size pieces. Combine the artichokes, mayonnaise and Parmesan cheese in a bowl and mix well. Spoon into a baking dish. Bake at 350 degrees for 25 minutes. Serve immediately.

roccoli Dip

1 (10-ounce) package frozen chopped
   broccoli
1 tablespoon butter
1 tablespoon flour
1 cup shredded Cheddar cheese

¹/2 cup sour cream
¹/2 teaspoon onion salt
¹/4 teaspoon lemon juice
¹/8 teaspoon pepper

Cook the broccoli using the package directions; drain. Melt the butter in a saucepan over medium heat. Add the flour and stir until smooth. Remove from the heat. Add the broccoli, Cheddar cheese, sour cream, onion salt, lemon juice and pepper and mix well. Spoon into a serving dish. Serve warm with wheat crackers.

ᒪ ayered Caviar Supreme

1 can chopped artichoke hearts, drained
4 eggs, hard-cooked, chopped
Mayonnaise to taste

4 green onions, chopped
1 can black caviar

Spread the artichokes in the bottom of a serving dish. Layer with the eggs, mayonnaise, green onions and caviar. Spread with enough additional mayonnaise to cover the caviar. Serve with wheat crackers.

even-Layer Mexican Dip

1 cup sour cream
1 envelope taco seasoning mix
1 large can chili with beans
1 cup guacamole or avocado dip

8 ounces shredded Cheddar cheese
1 can chopped black olives
1 bunch green onions, chopped
2 tomatoes, chopped

Mix sour cream and seasoning mix together. Layer the chili, seasoned sour cream, guacamole, Cheddar cheese, black olives, green onions and tomatoes in a serving dish. Serve with tortilla chips.

ot Chili Dip

2 pounds ground beef
2 pounds Velveeta cheese

Hot red pepper sauce to taste

Brown the ground beef in a skillet over medium heat, stirring until crumbly; drain. Add the Velveeta cheese and red pepper sauce to the skillet. Cook until the cheese is melted, stirring constantly. Spoon into a chafing dish. Serve warm with chips.

Cucumber Dip

2 large cucumbers
1/2 cup vinegar
1/2 teaspoon salt

16 ounces cream cheese
3/4 cup mayonnaise
1/2 teaspoon minced garlic

Grate the cucumbers on the 1/2-inch holes of a grater. Combine the cucumbers, vinegar and salt in a bowl and mix well. Chill, covered, for 8 to 10 hours. Drain the cucumbers and press to remove any excess moisture. Combine the cream cheese, mayonnaise and garlic in a bowl and mix well. Stir in the cucumbers. Spoon into a serving dish. Serve with favorite fresh vegetables.

Hot Seafood Dip

2 (14-ounce) cans artichoke hearts, drained and coarsely chopped
2 1/4 cups mayonnaise
2 cups grated Parmesan cheese

2 (6-ounce) cans lump crab meat, drained
1/3 cup seasoned bread crumbs
1 1/2 teaspoons garlic salt
1 teaspoon lemon pepper

Mix all the ingredients in a bowl. Spoon into a baking dish. Bake at 325 degrees for 20 to 25 minutes or until heated through. Serve warm or at room temperature with crackers.

Shrimp Dip

1 small can shrimp
8 ounces cream cheese, softened
1/2 cup mayonnaise

1/2 cup chopped celery
1/2 cup chopped green onions
2 tablespoons lemon juice

Combine the shrimp, cream cheese, mayonnaise, celery, green onions and lemon juice in a bowl and mix well. Spoon into a serving dish. Chill, covered, until serving time.

Spinach Dip

1 (10-ounce) package frozen chopped spinach
1 1/2 cups sour cream
1 cup mayonnaise

1 envelope vegetable soup mix
1 (8-ounce) can water chestnuts, chopped
3 green onions, chopped
1 loaf Hawaiian bread

Thaw the spinach and press to remove any excess moisture. Combine the sour cream, mayonnaise and soup mix in a bowl and mix well. Stir in the spinach, water chestnuts and green onions. Chill, covered, for 2 hours or longer. Cut a hole large enough to accommodate the dip in the center of the bread. Spoon the dip into the center of the bread. Serve immediately with pieces of the bread for dipping.

Spicy Spinach Fondue

1 (14-ounce) can artichoke hearts, drained, chopped
1 (12-ounce) jar salsa
1 (12-ounce) package frozen spinach soufflé, thawed
1 (9-ounce) package frozen creamed spinach, thawed
3/4 cup shredded Cheddar cheese
3/4 cup shredded mozzarella cheese

3/4 cup grated Parmesan cheese
2 tablespoons dried minced onion
1 teaspoon lemon pepper
1/2 teaspoon minced garlic
Sour cream to taste
2 tablespoons shredded Cheddar cheese
2 tablespoons shredded mozzarella cheese
2 tablespoons chopped green onions

Combine the artichoke hearts, 1/2 cup of the salsa, spinach soufflé, creamed spinach, 3/4 cup Cheddar cheese, 3/4 cup mozzarella cheese, Parmesan cheese, onion, lemon pepper and garlic in a large bowl and mix well. Spoon into a baking dish. Bake at 350 degrees for 25 to 30 minutes or until hot and bubbly. Top with sour cream, remaining salsa, 2 tablespoons Cheddar cheese, 2 tablespoons mozzarella cheese and green onions. Serve immediately with corn chips or tortilla chips.

Vegetable Dip

2 1/2 cups mayonnaise
1 1/2 cups sour cream
1 cup finely chopped onion
1 cup finely chopped green bell pepper

1/2 cup finely chopped pimentos
2 teaspoons salt
1/4 teaspoon Tabasco sauce
1/4 teaspoon garlic powder

Combine the mayonnaise, sour cream, onion, bell pepper, pimentos, salt, Tabasco sauce and garlic powder in a bowl and mix well. Spoon into a serving dish. Serve with crudités.

heese Ring

16 ounces extra-sharp Cheddar cheese, shredded
16 ounces medium Cheddar cheese, shredded
8 ounces cream cheese, softened

1 cup mayonnaise
1 medium onion, grated
1 teaspoon ground red pepper
Garlic salt to taste
1 cup chopped pecans

Combine the Cheddar cheese, cream cheese, mayonnaise, onion, red pepper and garlic salt in a large bowl and mix well. Grease a 7-cup mold. Sprinkle the pecans over the bottom of the mold. Press the cheese mixture into the mold. Chill, covered, until firm or for up to 24 hours. Unmold onto a serving plate. Serve with butter crackers and strawberry preserves.

imento Cheese Spread

2 cups shredded Cheddar cheese, at room temperature
4 ounces cream cheese, softened
1/2 cup mayonnaise
1 1/2 teaspoons lemon juice

1 teaspoon grated onion
1/4 teaspoon pepper
1 (4-ounce) jar sliced pimentos, drained and chopped

Combine the Cheddar cheese and cream cheese in a mixing bowl or food processor. Add the mayonnaise, lemon juice, onion and pepper. Beat or process until thoroughly mixed. Stir in the pimentos. Spoon into a serving dish. Chill, covered, until serving time. Let stand at room temperature for 15 minutes before serving. Serve with crackers or bread.

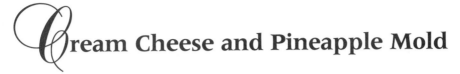

Cream Cheese and Pineapple Mold

1/2 cup chopped pecans
32 ounces cream cheese, softened
1 can crushed pineapple, drained

1/2 onion, chopped
1/2 green bell pepper, chopped

Spray a mold with nonstick spray. Sprinkle the pecans over the bottom of the mold. Combine the cream cheese, pineapple, onion and bell pepper in a bowl and mix well. Spoon into the prepared mold. Chill, covered, until set. Unmold onto a serving plate.

Hot Crab Spread

8 ounces cream cheese, softened
1 tablespoon milk
1 (6-ounce) can crab meat, drained and
  flaked

2 tablespoons finely chopped onion
1/2 to 3/4 teaspoon prepared horseradish
1/4 teaspoon salt
Dash of pepper

Combine the cream cheese and milk in a mixing bowl and beat until light and fluffy. Stir in the crab meat, onion, horseradish, salt and pepper. Spoon into a baking dish. Bake at 375 degrees for 15 minutes. Serve hot with crackers.

rab Pâté

1 (10-ounce) can cream of mushroom
    soup
1 envelope unflavored gelatin
3 tablespoons cold water
8 ounces cream cheese, softened

3/4 cup mayonnaise
1 (6-ounce) can crab meat, drained and
    flaked
1 small onion, grated
1 cup finely chopped celery

Heat the soup in a saucepan over low heat. Remove from the heat. Dissolve the gelatin in the cold water in a bowl. Stir into the heated soup. Add the cream cheese, mayonnaise, crab meat, onion and celery and mix well. Spoon into a mold. Chill, covered, until firm. Unmold onto a serving plate. Garnish with parsley. Serve with assorted crackers.

almon Mousse

2 envelopes unflavored gelatin
1/2 cup cold water
1 (15-ounce) can red salmon
1 1/2 cups whipping cream
1 cup mayonnaise
1 small onion, coarsely chopped

2 tablespoons cocktail sauce
1 tablespoon lemon juice
1/2 teaspoon garlic powder
1/2 teaspoon liquid smoke
Dash of white pepper
3 drops of hot red pepper sauce

Sprinkle the gelatin over the cold water in a saucepan. Let stand for 1 minute. Cook over low heat, stirring until the gelatin is dissolved. Drain the salmon; discard the skin and bones. Flake the salmon with a fork. Combine half each of the gelatin mixture, salmon, whipping cream, mayonnaise and onion in a blender or food processor. Process until smooth. Spoon the salmon mixture into a bowl. Repeat the procedure with the remaining gelatin mixture, salmon, whipping cream, mayonnaise and onion. Add the cocktail sauce, lemon juice, garlic powder, liquid smoke, white pepper and red pepper sauce to the salmon mixture and mix well. Spoon into a lightly oiled 5-cup fish or shell-shaped mold. Chill, covered, for 8 hours or longer. Unmold onto a lettuce-lined serving plate. Garnish with sliced cucumber and pimento-stuffed olives. Serve with assorted crackers.

$\mathscr{S}$hrimp Christmas Tree

1 1/2 cups ketchup
2 tablespoons prepared horseradish
1 tablespoon lemon juice
1 tablespoon Worcestershire sauce
1 1/2 teaspoons sugar
Dash of hot red pepper sauce
Salt and pepper to taste

1 1/2 quarts water
1/3 cup salt
2 pounds fresh or frozen medium shrimp
3 bunches curly endive
1 (1 1/2-foot-high) Styrofoam cone
1 small box round wooden picks

Combine the ketchup, horseradish, lemon juice, Worcestershire sauce, sugar, red pepper sauce, salt and pepper to taste in a bowl and mix well. Chill, covered, until serving time.

Combine the water and 1/3 cup salt in a saucepan. Bring to a boil over medium-high heat. Add the shrimp. Reduce the heat to low. Simmer, covered, for 5 minutes or until the shrimp are pink and tender; drain. Peel and devein the shrimp, leaving the tail section of the shell intact. Chill until serving time. Separate the leaves of the curly endive. Chill until serving time. Cover the Styrofoam cone with the curly endive, starting at the bottom and working up and using wooden pick halves to attach the leaves to the cone. Attach the shrimp to the tree using wooden picks. Serve the shrimp with the cocktail sauce.

$\mathscr{S}$hrimp Mold

1 envelope unflavored gelatin
1/4 cup warm water
1 can tomato soup
8 ounces cream cheese
1 cup mayonnaise

1/2 cup finely chopped green bell pepper
1/2 cup finely chopped onion
1/2 cup finely chopped celery
2 cups chopped boiled shrimp

Dissolve the gelatin in the warm water in a bowl. Combine the soup and cream cheese in a saucepan. Cook over low heat until cream cheese is melted, stirring frequently. Remove from the heat. Combine the gelatin mixture, soup mixture and mayonnaise in a bowl and mix well. Stir in the bell pepper, onion, celery and shrimp. Spoon into a mold. Chill, covered, until set. Unmold onto a serving plate.

heese Petits Fours

2 cups (4 sticks) butter, softened
4 jars Old English cheese spread
1 1/2 teaspoons Worcestershire sauce
1 teaspoon Tabasco sauce

1 teaspoon onion powder
3 loaves thinly sliced bread
Cayenne pepper to taste
Dillseeds to taste

Combine the butter, cheese spread, Worcestershire sauce, Tabasco sauce and onion powder in a mixing bowl and beat until of the consistency of frosting. Cut the crusts from 3 slices of bread. Spread butter mixture between the slices. Cut into quarters. Spread cheese over the top and sides of each petit four. Arrange on a baking sheet. Repeat the procedure with the remaining bread and butter mixture. Freeze the petits fours until firm. Store in plastic bags in the freezer until ready to bake. Bake on a baking sheet at 350 degrees for 15 to 20 minutes. Sprinkle with cayenne pepper and dillseeds.

exican Tortilla Pinwheels

8 ounces cream cheese, softened
1 small can chopped green chiles, drained
1 jar picante sauce, drained

Minced garlic to taste
1 package flour tortillas, at room
 temperature

Beat the cream cheese in a mixing bowl until smooth. Fold in the green chiles, picante sauce and garlic. Spread equal portions of the cream cheese mixture over the tortillas. Roll to enclose the filling. Freeze, wrapped in plastic wrap, until ready to serve. Remove from the freezer and let stand until partially thawed. Cut into slices. Serve on a platter with additional picante sauce.

Swiss and Parmesan Bruschetta

1 1/2 cups shredded Swiss cheese
1/4 cup grated Parmesan cheese
1/4 cup cottage cheese
1/4 cup mayonnaise

2 ounces cream cheese, softened
1/4 cup chopped green onions
1 loaf French bread

Combine the Swiss cheese, Parmesan cheese, cottage cheese, mayonnaise, cream cheese and green onions in a bowl and mix well. Slice the French bread into 1/2-inch-thick slices. Toast until golden brown. Spread the toasted slices with the cheese mixture. Broil on a baking sheet for 4 to 5 minutes or until bubbly and light brown. Serve warm.

Oriental Chicken Wings

48 chicken wings
1 cup honey
3/4 cup soy sauce

1/2 cup grated fresh gingerroot
1/4 cup minced garlic
Lightly toasted sesame seeds to taste

Arrange the chicken wings in a single layer in baking pans. Combine the honey, soy sauce, gingerroot and garlic in a bowl and mix well. Spoon evenly over the chicken wings. Bake at 350 degrees for 45 minutes or until the chicken is cooked through and brown and the coating is thickened. Sprinkle with sesame seeds. Serve hot or at room temperature.

am Rolls

1/2 cup (1 stick) butter, softened	2 teaspoons Worcestershire sauce
1 small onion, grated	1 (20-count) package party rolls
2 tablespoons poppy seeds	1 (4-ounce) package sliced cooked ham
2 teaspoons prepared mustard	1 (4-ounce) package sliced Swiss cheese

Combine the butter, onion, poppy seeds, mustard and Worcestershire sauce in a bowl and mix well. Slice the whole set of rolls in half horizontally. Return the bottom half of the rolls to the foil pan. Arrange the ham and Swiss cheese evenly over the bottom half of the rolls. Spread the butter mixture over the inside of the top half of the rolls. Place butter side down on top of the Swiss cheese. Bake at 350 degrees until the Swiss cheese is melted. May be chilled or frozen, wrapped in foil, before baking.

ausage Balls

1 pound hot or mild bulk pork sausage	2 cups shredded Cheddar cheese
3 cups baking mix	

Combine sausage, baking mix and Cheddar cheese in a bowl and mix well, adding a small amount of water if mixture seems dry. Shape into 1-inch balls. Bake at 350 degrees for 15 minutes; drain on paper towels. Serve warm. May freeze, covered, before or after baking.

ausage Snack Wraps

2 (8-count) cans crescent rolls	48 cocktail smoked sausage links

Separate each package of crescent roll dough into 8 triangles. Cut each triangle lengthwise into thirds. Place a sausage on the short side of each triangle. Roll up from the short side to the opposite point. Bake at 375 degrees for 12 to 15 minutes or until golden brown. Serve warm. May be chilled, covered, for up to 2 hours before baking.

# Cocktail Franks with Bourbon

1 cup bourbon
1 cup ketchup
1/2 cup packed brown sugar
2 tablespoons chopped onion

2 teaspoons Worcestershire sauce
1/8 teaspoon Tabasco sauce
1 package cocktail franks

Combine the bourbon, ketchup, brown sugar, onion, Worcestershire sauce and Tabasco sauce in a saucepan. Cook over medium heat for 30 minutes. Arrange the franks in a baking dish. Spoon the bourbon mixture over the franks. Bake at 325 degrees for 1 hour.

# Shrimp Puffs

1 egg white
1/2 cup mayonnaise
1/4 cup grated cheese
1/8 teaspoon salt
1/8 teaspoon paprika

Dash of ground red pepper
24 bread rounds, toasted
12 shrimp, cooked, peeled, cut into
  halves

Beat the egg white in a mixing bowl until stiff peaks form. Fold in the mayonnaise, cheese, salt, paprika and red pepper. Spoon equal portions of the mayonnaise mixture onto the bread rounds. Top each with a shrimp half and place on a baking sheet. Broil under moderate heat until light brown. Serve immediately.

Vegetable Bars

2 (8-count) cans crescent rolls
16 ounces cream cheese, softened
1 cup mayonnaise
1 envelope ranch salad dressing mix
1/2 head cauliflower, chopped

1 stalk broccoli, chopped
1 green bell pepper, chopped
2 medium carrots, grated
1 1/2 cups shredded Cheddar cheese

Unroll the crescent roll dough and press the perforations to seal. Pat onto the bottom and sides of a 10×15-inch baking pan. Bake at 350 degrees for 10 minutes or until golden brown. Let stand to cool completely. Combine the cream cheese, mayonnaise and salad dressing mix in a bowl and mix well. Spread over the cooled crust. Arrange the cauliflower, broccoli, bell pepper and carrots over the cream cheese layer and pat lightly. Sprinkle with the Cheddar cheese. Cut into small bars. May substitute other vegetables for the cauliflower, broccoli, bell pepper and carrots.

Cheese Straws

2 1/2 cups flour
1 cup shredded sharp Cheddar cheese
1 cup shredded mild Cheddar cheese
1 cup (2 sticks) butter, softened

1 1/2 teaspoons salt
1/2 teaspoon garlic salt
1/2 teaspoon pepper

Combine the flour, Cheddar cheese, butter, salt, garlic salt and pepper in a bowl and mix well. Place the dough in a cookie press or pastry tube. Press 2-inch straws onto a nonstick baking sheet. Bake at 350 degrees for 10 to 12 minutes or until set; do not brown. Cool on the baking sheet for 2 minutes. Remove to a wire rack to cool completely.

Crispy Cheese Wafers

2 cups shredded sharp Cheddar cheese
1 cup (2 sticks) margarine, softened
2 cups flour

2 cups crisp rice cereal
Cayenne pepper to taste (optional)

Combine the Cheddar cheese and margarine in a mixing bowl and beat until well mixed. Beat in the flour gradually. Fold in the cereal and cayenne pepper. Shape into small balls. Arrange on an ungreased baking sheet. Flatten with a fork. Bake at 375 degrees for 8 to 10 minutes or until crisp; do not brown. Cool on the baking sheet for 2 minutes. Remove to a wire rack to cool completely. Store in an airtight container at room temperature or freeze for future use.

Party Mix

1/2 cup (1 stick) butter or margarine
4 1/2 teaspoons Worcestershire sauce
1 1/4 teaspoons seasoned salt
2 cups Chex corn cereal

2 cups Chex rice cereal
2 cups Chex bran cereal
2 cups Chex wheat cereal
1 cup salted mixed nuts

Place the butter in a 10×15-inch baking pan. Heat in a 250-degree oven until the butter is melted. Stir in the Worcestershire sauce and seasoned salt. Add the cereal and mixed nuts and stir until coated with the butter mixture. Bake for 1 hour, stirring every 15 minutes. Spread on paper towels to cool. Store in an airtight container. May be frozen for future use.

Trash

1 box Cheerios
1 box Chex wheat cereal or bite-size
   shredded wheat cereal
1 package thin pretzels (optional)

3 cups mixed nuts
1¹/₂ cups (3 sticks) margarine, melted
1 tablespoon garlic salt
1 tablespoon Worcestershire sauce

Combine the Cheerios, cereal, pretzels and mixed nuts in a bowl and mix well. Combine the margarine, garlic salt and Worcestershire sauce in a bowl and mix well. Pour over the cereal mixture and stir until the cereal mixture is coated. Arrange in a 10×15-inch baking pan. Bake at 200 degrees for 1 hour, stirring frequently.

Popcorn Delight

8 cups popped popcorn
3 cups corn chips, coarsely crushed
2 cups crispy corn puffs cereal

1 pound white chocolate, chopped
2 cups candy-coated chocolate pieces
   (optional)

Combine the popcorn, corn chips and cereal in a bowl and mix well. Place the white chocolate in a microwave-safe bowl. Microwave on High until melted, stirring once every minute. Drizzle over the popcorn mixture and toss to coat. Fold in the candy-coated chocolate pieces. Spread on a waxed-paper-lined 10×15-inch pan. Chill for 30 minutes. Break into pieces. Store in an airtight container.

Sweet and Spicy Pecans

1 cup warm water
1/4 cup sugar
1 cup pecan halves

2 tablespoons sugar
1 tablespoon chili powder
1/8 teaspoon ground red pepper

Combine the warm water and 1/4 cup sugar in a bowl and stir until the sugar is dissolved. Stir in the pecans. Let stand for 10 minutes; drain. Combine 2 tablespoons sugar, chili powder and red pepper in a bowl and mix well. Add the pecans and toss to coat. Arrange the pecans on a lightly greased baking sheet. Bake at 350 degrees for 10 minutes, stirring frequently.

Glazed Pecans

1 cup sugar
1/2 cup water
1 1/2 teaspoons vanilla extract

1 teaspoon cinnamon
3/4 teaspoon salt
1 pound pecan halves

Combine the sugar and water in a small saucepan. Cook over medium heat until the sugar is dissolved, stirring frequently. Add the vanilla, cinnamon and salt and mix well. Bring to a boil. Boil until mixture reaches 236 degrees on a candy thermometer, soft-ball stage, stirring constantly. Arrange on waxed paper. Let stand to cool completely. Break into pieces.

Candy-Coated Nuts

1 cup packed brown sugar
1/2 cup each sugar and sour cream

1 teaspoon vanilla extract
2 1/2 cups pecan halves or walnuts

Combine the brown sugar, sugar and sour cream in a saucepan. Cook over medium heat to 236 degrees on a candy thermometer, soft-ball stage. Add the vanilla and beat until the mixture begins to thicken. Add the pecans and stir until coated. Spread on a greased platter or baking sheet. Let stand to cool completely. Break into pieces.

Butter Mints

4 ounces cream cheese, softened
1/4 cup (1/2 stick) butter or margarine
11/2 pounds confectioners' sugar

4 drops of peppermint extract
3 drops of mint extract
Food coloring to taste

Combine all the ingredients in a bowl and mix well. Press into molds. Chill, covered, until set. Unmold onto a plate.

Lobster Bisque

4 cans lobster bisque soup
16 ounces cream cheese
1 pound white crab meat, flaked

1/2 cup chopped celery
1/2 cup chopped onion

Cook the soup using the package directions. Add the cream cheese, crab meat, celery and onion. Cook over medium heat until heated through, stirring frequently. Serve with toast points.

Cream of Potato Soup

2 to 4 large potatoes, chopped
1 large onion, chopped
1 carrot, grated (optional)
2 tablespoons margarine

2 tablespoons flour
21/2 cups milk
1/2 cup evaporated milk

Combine the potatoes, onion and carrot in a saucepan. Add enough water to cover. Cook over medium heat until the potatoes are tender; drain. Melt the margarine in a saucepan over medium heat. Add the flour and stir until smooth. Add the milk and evaporated milk gradually, stirring constantly. Cook until mixture begins to thicken, stirring frequently. Stir in the potato mixture. Cook until heated through. Ladle into soup bowls. Garnish with chopped fresh parsley or chives.

anana Punch

6 cups water
4 cups sugar
2 (16-ounce) cans frozen orange juice
   concentrate, thawed
1 (12-ounce) can frozen lemonade
   concentrate, thawed

1 (46-ounce) can pineapple juice
6 bananas, mashed
4 to 5 bottles ginger ale or lemon-lime
   soda

Combine the water and sugar in a saucepan. Bring to a boil over medium-high heat, stirring to dissolve the sugar. Let stand to cool. Add the orange juice concentrate, lemonade concentrate, pineapple juice and bananas and mix well. Freeze in two 1-gallon jugs. Remove from the freezer 2 hours before serving time. Let stand at room temperature to thaw. Pour into a punch bowl. Add the ginger ale and mix well.

piced Cranberry Cider

1 quart apple cider
3 cups cranberry juice cocktail
2 to 3 tablespoons brown sugar

2 sticks cinnamon
3/4 teaspoon whole cloves
1/2 lemon, thinly sliced

Combine the apple cider, cranberry juice, brown sugar, cinnamon, cloves and lemon in a Dutch oven and mix well. Bring to a boil over medium-high heat, stirring frequently. Reduce the heat to low. Cook for 15 to 20 minutes. Remove cinnamon sticks and cloves. Ladle into mugs. Garnish with additional cinnamon sticks.

 Hot Perky Punch

2 quarts cranberry juice cocktail
2 quarts pineapple juice
1 quart water
1¹/2 cups packed brown sugar

1 tablespoon whole allspice
1 tablespoon whole cloves
2 or 3 lemon slices
4 sticks cinnamon

Combine the cranberry juice, pineapple juice and water in a 36-cup coffee urn. Place the brown sugar, allspice, cloves, lemon and cinnamon in the basket of the urn. Perk using the coffee urn directions.

 Christmas Punch

1 envelope lime drink mix
1 quart pineapple juice

1 quart lime sherbet
2 quarts ginger ale

Prepare the drink mix in a punch bowl using the package directions. Add the pineapple juice. Add the sherbet by scoopfuls. Stir in the ginger ale. May use raspberry drink mix and sherbet in place of the lime drink mix and sherbet.

Holiday Punch

4 cups water
3¹/2 cups sugar
2 quarts pineapple juice
2 quarts cranberry juice cocktail

Juice of 1 lemon
2 tablespoons almond extract
4 quarts ginger ale

Combine the water and sugar in a saucepan. Bring to a boil over medium-high heat. Cook until the sugar is dissolved, stirring constantly. Remove from the heat. Add the pineapple juice, cranberry juice, lemon juice and almond extract and mix well. Freeze in a covered bowl until serving time. Place frozen punch in a punch bowl. Add the ginger ale. Garnish with apple slices.

rape Punch

1 (12-ounce) can frozen
orange juice concentrate
1 (12-ounce) can frozen grape juice
concentrate
1 (12-ounce) can frozen pink lemonade
concentrate

1 cup sugar
1 (46-ounce) can sweetened pineapple
juice
1 liter ginger ale

Prepare the orange juice, grape juice and pink lemonade in a large bowl using the package directions, reserving 1 cup of the water. Combine the reserved water and sugar in a saucepan. Cook over medium heat until the sugar is dissolved, stirring constantly. Let stand until cool. Combine the orange juice, grape juice, pink lemonade, pineapple juice, ginger ale and sugar mixture in a punch bowl and mix well.

each Punch

1 (10-ounce) can frozen peach daiquiri
mix concentrate
1 (12-ounce) can frozen peach medley
juice concentrate

1 (12-ounce) can pineapple-orange-
banana juice concentrate
60 ounces water
1 liter ginger ale

Combine the daiquiri mix concentrate, peach medley juice concentrate, pineapple-orange-banana juice concentrate and water in a punch bowl and mix well. Chill, covered, until serving time. Add the ginger ale just before serving.

lush Punch

4 (3-ounce) packages strawberry
  gelatin
4 cups sugar
5 cups hot water
1 (6-ounce) can frozen orange juice
  concentrate, thawed

1 (6-ounce) can frozen limeade
  concentrate, thawed
2 (46-ounce) cans pineapple juice
1 ounce almond extract
1 1/2 gallons cold water
2 to 3 liters lemon-lime soda

Dissolve the gelatin and sugar in the hot water in a bowl. Stir in the orange juice concentrate, limeade concentrate, pineapple juice, almond extract and cold water. Freeze in gallon jugs. Cut the bottom from one of the jugs. Cut shavings of the punch into the punch bowl using a sharp knife. Add 1 liter of the soda. Repeat procedure as needed. May use different flavors of gelatin.

Sparkling Red Punch

1 (16-ounce) can pineapple juice, chilled
1 (16-ounce) can frozen orange juice
  concentrate, thawed
1 (16-ounce) can frozen lemon juice
  concentrate, thawed
2 cups cold water

2 packages unsweetened strawberry drink
  mix
1 quart lemon sherbet
1 (12-ounce) bottle strawberry soda,
  chilled
1 quart carbonated water, chilled

Combine the pineapple juice, orange juice concentrate, lemon juice concentrate, cold water and drink mix in a punch bowl and mix well. Add the sherbet. Stir in the soda and carbonated water just before serving.

Salads

 pple Almond Salad

1/4 cup vegetable oil
2 tablespoons sugar
2 tablespoons red wine vinegar
1/4 teaspoon each salt and almond extract

1 to 2 medium Granny Smith apples, sliced
1 cup thinly sliced leaf lettuce or romaine
2 tablespoons sliced green onions
1/3 cup toasted slivered almonds

For the salad dressing, combine the first 5 ingredients in a bowl and mix well. Chill, covered, for several hours. For the salad, combine the apples, lettuce, green onions and almonds in a salad bowl. Pour the salad dressing over the salad and toss to mix. Serve immediately.

 aldorf Salad

1 cup each mayonnaise and sour cream
2 tablespoons honey
3 cups chopped tart apples

2 cups halved seedless red grapes
2 cups chopped celery
1 cup chopped walnuts

For the salad dressing, combine the mayonnaise, sour cream, and honey in a bowl and mix well. For the salad, combine the apples, grapes, celery and walnuts in a salad bowl. Pour the salad dressing over the salad and toss to mix. Serve immediately.

ing Cherry Salad

1 (16-ounce) can Bing cherries
1 (20-ounce) can crushed pineapple
2 (3-ounce) packages cherry gelatin

1 (12-ounce) can Coca-Cola
1 cup chopped nuts (optional)

Drain the cherries and pineapple, reserving 2 cups juice. Chop the cherries. Heat the reserved juice in a saucepan over medium heat. Pour heated juice over the gelatin. Stir until gelatin is dissolved; cool. Stir in the Coca-Cola. Chill until partially set. Stir in the cherries, pineapple and nuts. Spoon into a dish. Chill, covered, until set.

ink Cherry Salad

1 (20-ounce) can crushed pineapple, drained
1 (21-ounce) can cherry pie filling
1 large container whipped topping
1 (14-ounce) can sweetened condensed milk
1 cup chopped nuts
1/3 cup lemon juice

Combine the pineapple, pie filling, whipped topping, sweetened condensed milk, nuts and lemon juice in a bowl and mix well. Spoon into a serving dish. Chill, covered, until set. May also be spooned into paper-lined muffin tins and frozen. Serve on a bed of leaf lettuce.

ranberry Orange Salad

1 (16-ounce) can crushed pineapple
1/2 cup water
1 (6-ounce) package orange gelatin
1 (16-ounce) can cranberry sauce
1 cup chopped nuts
Grated zest of 1 orange

Drain the pineapple, reserving 1/2 cup of the juice. Combine the reserved juice and water in a saucepan. Cook over medium heat until heated through. Add the gelatin and stir until dissolved. Crush the cranberry sauce in a bowl. Add to the gelatin mixture and mix well. Stir in the nuts and orange zest. Spoon into a mold. Chill, covered, until set.

ranberry Congealed Salad

1 (20-ounce) can crushed pineapple
2 (3-ounce) packages cherry gelatin
1 (16-ounce) can whole cranberry sauce
1 (11-ounce) can mandarin oranges, drained
1/3 cup chopped nuts

Drain the pineapple, reserving the juice. Cook the reserved juice in a saucepan over medium heat until heated through. Add the gelatin and stir until dissolved. Stir in the cranberry sauce and pineapple. Fold in the oranges and nuts. Spoon into a glass dish. Chill, covered, until set.

mbrosia Salad

1 cup hot water
1/2 cup sugar
1 (3-ounce) package orange gelatin
3 oranges, cut into bite-size pieces

1 small can crushed pineapple, drained
1 cup shredded coconut
1 cup chopped nuts
1 cup sour cream

Combine the hot water, sugar and gelatin in a bowl and stir until the gelatin and sugar is dissolved. Stir in the oranges, pineapple, coconut, nuts and sour cream. Spoon into a serving dish. Chill, covered, until set.

Creamy Orange Fruit Salad

1 (4-ounce) package vanilla instant
    pudding mix
1 1/2 cups milk
1/3 cup frozen orange juice concentrate,
    thawed
3/4 cup sour cream

1 (20-ounce) can pineapple tidbits,
    drained
1 (15-ounce) can sliced peaches, drained
1 (11-ounce) can mandarin oranges
2 bananas, sliced
1 apple, peeled, cored, sliced

For the salad dressing, combine the pudding mix, milk and orange juice concentrate in a mixing bowl. Beat at medium speed for 2 1/2 minutes. Add the sour cream and mix well. For the salad, combine the pineapple, peaches, mandarin oranges, bananas and apple in a salad bowl. Spoon the salad dressing over the salad and mix gently. Chill, covered, for 3 hours.

Orange Sherbet Salad

2 (3-ounce) packages orange gelatin
1 cup boiling water
1 pint orange sherbet
1 (11-ounce) can mandarin oranges,
    drained

1 (8-ounce) can crushed pineapple,
    drained
1 cup miniature marshmallows
1 cup whipping cream, whipped, or
    8 ounces whipped topping

Dissolve the gelatin in the boiling water in a bowl. Add the sherbet and mix well. Chill, covered, until partially set. Stir in the mandarin oranges, pineapple and marshmallows. Fold in the whipped cream. Spoon into a serving dish. Chill, covered, until set.

Orange Congealed Salad

2 (6-ounce) packages orange gelatin
4 cups boiling water
1 (20-ounce) can crushed pineapple
1 can mandarin oranges

1 (3-ounce) package lemon instant
    pudding mix
1 cup milk
1 large container whipped topping

Dissolve the gelatin in the boiling water in a bowl. Stir in the undrained pineapple. Drain the mandarin oranges, reserving the juice. Cut the mandarin oranges into halves. Add the mandarin oranges and reserved juice to the gelatin mixture and mix well. Spoon into a serving dish. Chill, covered, until set. Prepare the pudding mix according to package directions, using 1 cup milk. Fold in the whipped topping. Spread over the top of the salad. Chill, covered, until set.

ear Salad

1 (3-ounce) package peach gelatin
1 cup boiling water
1 medium can sliced pears

3 ounces cream cheese, softened
8 ounces whipped topping

Combine the gelatin and boiling water in a bowl and stir until the gelatin is dissolved. Drain the pears, reserving the juice in a 1-cup measure. Add enough water to the pear juice to measure 3/4 cup. Add to the gelatin mixture and mix well. Mash the pears in a bowl. Add the cream cheese and mix well. Stir in the gelatin mixture and whipped topping. Spoon into a serving dish. Chill, covered, until set.

loud Nine Cream

1 (8-ounce) can crushed pineapple
8 ounces cream cheese, softened
1 (2-ounce) package whipped
  topping mix

1/2 cup chopped pecans
1/2 cup drained maraschino cherries
3 tablespoons sugar

Drain the pineapple, reserving 1/4 cup of the juice. Place the cream cheese in a mixing bowl and beat until creamy. Add the reserved juice gradually, beating constantly. Beat until light and smooth. Prepare the whipped topping mix using the package directions. Fold in the cream cheese mixture, pineapple, pecans, maraschino cherries and sugar. Chill, covered, for 3 hours.

$\mathcal{S}$trawberry Banana Congealed Salad

2 packages strawberry gelatin
2 cups boiling water
2 (10-ounce) packages frozen
    strawberries

1 (8-ounce) can crushed pineapple
2 large bananas, mashed
1 cup chopped pecans
1 cup sour cream

Dissolve the gelatin in the boiling water in a bowl. Add the strawberries and stir until the strawberries are thawed. Stir in the pineapple, bananas and pecans. Spoon half the gelatin mixture into an 8×8-inch dish. Chill, covered, until set. Spread with the sour cream. Spoon the remaining gelatin mixture over the sour cream. Chill, covered, until set. Cut into squares.

$\mathcal{F}$rozen Fruit Salad

1 quart strawberry ice cream, softened
8 ounces cream cheese, softened
1/2 cup mayonnaise-type salad dressing

2 (No. 1) cans fruit cocktail, drained
1/3 cup chopped pecans

Mix the first 3 ingredients in a bowl. Stir in the fruit cocktail and pecans. Spoon into a 9×9-inch dish. Freeze, covered, until firm. Cut into squares and serve on beds of lettuce.

$\mathcal{M}$other's Finest Chicken Salad

6 boneless skinless chicken breast halves
1/2 cup chopped celery
1/2 cup slivered almonds

2 cups Hellman's mayonnaise
1/2 teaspoon salt
1/2 teaspoon pepper

Combine the chicken with enough water to cover in a saucepan. Cook over medium heat until cooked through. Chop coarsely. Process in a food processor until chopped. Process the celery and almonds separately in a food processor until chopped. Spoon into a bowl. Stir in the mayonnaise, salt and pepper. Serve immediately or chill, covered, until serving time.

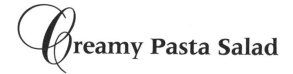reamy Pasta Salad

1 (16-ounce) package rotini
1/2 cup mayonnaise
1/2 cup French salad dressing
1 cucumber, chopped

1/2 medium onion, chopped
1/2 green bell pepper, chopped
1/4 cup chopped red bell pepper
1 teaspoon seasoned salt

Cook the pasta using the package directions; drain. Combine the pasta, mayonnaise, salad dressing, cucumber, onion, bell peppers and seasoned salt in a bowl and mix well. Spoon into a serving dish. Serve immediately or chill, covered, until serving time.

oppy Seed Pasta Salad

8 ounces shell pasta
1/2 cup chopped celery
1/2 cup chopped green onions
1/2 cup chopped tomatoes

1/2 cup chopped green bell pepper
3/4 cup grated Parmesan cheese
Poppy seeds to taste
Italian salad dressing

Cook the pasta using the package directions; drain. Combine the pasta, celery, green onions, tomatoes, bell pepper, Parmesan cheese and poppy seeds in a salad bowl. Add enough salad dressing to moisten and toss to mix. Chill, covered, until serving time. Serve cold.

oppy Seed Salad Dressing

2 cups vegetable oil
3/4 cup honey
3/4 cup vinegar
1 small onion, grated

6 tablespoons prepared mustard
5 tablespoons poppy seeds
1 1/2 teaspoons salt

Combine the vegetable oil, honey, vinegar, onion, mustard, poppy seeds and salt in a blender. Process until mixture is blended and thickened.

runchy California Salad

1/4 cup vegetable oil
2 tablespoons sugar
2 tablespoons red wine vinegar
1/4 teaspoon salt
1/4 teaspoon almond extract

1 package California salad mix
1 small can mandarin oranges
10 to 12 strawberries, quartered
1/2 cup Chinese noodles
Sweet and Spicy Nuts

For the salad dressing, combine the vegetable oil, sugar, vinegar, salt and almond extract in a bowl and mix well. For the salad, combine the salad mix, oranges, strawberries, Chinese noodles and Sweet and Spicy Nuts in a salad bowl. Pour the salad dressing over the salad and toss lightly to mix.

Sweet and Spicy Nuts

1 egg white
1/2 cup packed light brown sugar

Cayenne pepper to taste
1/2 cup pecan halves

Place the egg white in a mixing bowl and beat until foamy. Combine the brown sugar and cayenne pepper in a bowl and mix well. Coat the pecans with the beaten egg white. Add to the brown sugar mixture and toss to coat. Arrange on a baking sheet. Bake at 325 degrees for 20 minutes or until light brown.

wenty-Four Hour Salad

1 head lettuce
1 tablespoon sugar
1 bunch green onions, sliced
1 (6-ounce) can sliced water chestnuts, drained
1 cup chopped celery

1/2 (10-ounce) package frozen green peas
2 cups Hellman's mayonnaise
1/2 cup grated Parmesan cheese
Chopped hard-cooked eggs
Bacon bits
Chopped tomatoes

Tear the lettuce into bite-size pieces and place in a 9×11-inch glass dish. Sprinkle with the sugar. Layer with the green onions, water chestnuts, celery and green peas. Spread with the mayonnaise. Sprinkle with Parmesan cheese. Chill, covered, for 24 hours. Top with eggs, bacon bits and tomatoes just before serving.

ot Bean Salad

3 or 4 slices bacon
2/3 cup vinegar
1/2 cup sugar
1 tablespoon cornstarch
1 teaspoon salt
1/4 teaspoon pepper

1 medium onion, chopped
2 cups drained canned cut green beans
1 (16-ounce) can cut green wax beans, drained
1 can red kidney beans, drained

Cook the bacon in a skillet over medium heat until crisp. Remove to paper towels to drain. Add the vinegar, sugar, cornstarch, salt and pepper to the pan drippings in the skillet. Cook until the mixture comes to a boil, stirring constantly. Reduce the heat to low. Add the onion, green beans, wax beans and kidney beans and mix well. Cook for 20 to 25 minutes. Spoon into a serving dish. Crumble the bacon. Sprinkle over the top of the salad. Serve immediately.

Broccoli Salad

1 cup mayonnaise
1/4 cup sugar
1 tablespoon lemon juice
1 large bunch broccoli, chopped

1 small red onion, chopped
1/2 cup raisins
1/2 cup chopped pecans
6 to 8 slices bacon, crisp-fried, crumbled

Combine the mayonnaise, sugar and lemon juice in a bowl and mix well. Combine the broccoli, onion, raisins, pecans and bacon in a salad bowl and mix well. Add the mayonnaise mixture and toss gently to mix. Chill, covered, for 2 to 3 hours.

Oriental Salad

2 (3-ounce) packages ramen noodles
1 small package sunflower seeds
1 small package slivered almonds
1/4 cup (1/2 stick) margarine, melted
1 medium head cabbage, chopped
6 green onions, or 1 medium onion,
    chopped

1 cup sugar
1 cup vegetable oil
1/2 cup apple cider vinegar
2 tablespoons soy sauce

Break the ramen noodles into a bowl; discard the seasoning packets. Add the sunflower seeds and almonds and mix well. Pour the margarine over the noodle mixture and mix well. Spread the mixture on a baking sheet. Bake at 350 degrees for 10 to 15 minutes, turning after 6 minutes; do not overbrown. Let stand to cool. Combine the cabbage and green onions in a bowl. Combine the sugar, vegetable oil, vinegar and soy sauce in a bowl and whisk until well mixed. Pour over the cabbage mixture. Combine the cabbage mixture and noodle mixture in a salad bowl and toss lightly to mix. Serve immediately.

Special Coleslaw

1 large head cabbage, shredded
3 carrots, shredded
1 red bell pepper, slivered
1 green bell pepper, slivered
1 medium onion, chopped
1 cup sugar

1/2 cup balsamic vinegar
1/2 cup white vinegar
2 tablespoons vegetable oil
2 teaspoons salt
2 teaspoons hot dry mustard
1 teaspoon celery seeds

Combine the cabbage, carrots, bell peppers and onion in a salad bowl and mix well. Combine the sugar, balsamic vinegar, white vinegar, vegetable oil, salt, mustard and celery seeds in a bowl and mix well. Pour over the cabbage mixture and mix well. Chill, covered, until serving time.

Crunchy Pea Salad

3/4 cup water
1 teaspoon sugar
1 pound shelled fresh sweet green peas
1 cup chopped cauliflower
1 cup cashews, chopped

2 ribs celery, chopped
6 green onions, sliced
1 cup ranch salad dressing
1/2 cup sour cream
8 slices bacon, crisp-fried, crumbled

Combine the water and sugar in a saucepan. Bring to a boil over medium-high heat, stirring constantly to dissolve the sugar. Add the peas and cook for 10 minutes; drain. Combine the peas, cauliflower, cashews, celery, green onions, salad dressing and sour cream in a bowl and mix well. Spoon into a salad bowl. Chill, covered, for 1 hour. Sprinkle with the bacon. Serve immediately.

Mother's Finest Potato Salad

5 pounds potatoes, scrubbed
2 cups Hellman's mayonnaise
8 eggs, hard-cooked, finely chopped
1 cup chopped sweet pickle relish

1/2 cup (1 stick) margarine, melted
1/2 cup chopped pimentos
Salt and pepper to taste

Combine the potatoes and enough water to cover in a saucepan. Cook over medium heat until tender; drain. Let stand to cool. Peel and chop the potatoes. Combine the potatoes, mayonnaise, eggs, pickle relish, margarine, pimentos, salt and pepper in a bowl and mix well. Spoon into a glass serving dish. Serve on beds of lettuce.

Marinated Tomatoes

3 very large ripe tomatoes
1/3 cup olive oil
1/4 cup sherry wine vinegar or red wine
   vinegar
1/4 cup finely chopped onion
2 tablespoons drained capers

2 tablespoons finely chopped fresh
   parsley
1 large garlic clove, minced
1 teaspoon dried basil
1 teaspoon salt
1/4 teaspoon pepper

Cut the tomatoes into 1/2-inch-thick slices. Arrange in a single layer in a shallow dish. Combine the olive oil, vinegar, onion, capers, parsley, garlic, basil, salt and pepper in a bowl and mix well. Spoon over the tomatoes. Chill, covered, for 3 hours. Garnish with parsley sprigs.

Parmesan Vegetable Toss

2 cups mayonnaise
1/2 cup grated Parmesan cheese
1/4 cup sugar
1/2 teaspoon dried basil
1/2 teaspoon salt
2 cups broccoli florets
2 cups cauliflower florets

1 (6-ounce) can sliced water chestnuts, drained
1/2 cup chopped red onion
1 head lettuce, shredded
Croutons
Bacon, crisp-fried, crumbled

Combine the mayonnaise, Parmesan cheese, sugar, basil and salt in a bowl and mix well. Combine the broccoli, cauliflower, water chestnuts and red onion in a bowl and mix well. Add the mayonnaise mixture and toss to mix well. Place the lettuce in the bottom of a serving dish. Add the broccoli mixture. Top with the croutons and bacon. Serve immediately.

Marinated Vegetables

1 cup cauliflower florets
1 cup broccoli florets
1 cup chopped zucchini
1 cup chopped carrots
1 cup chopped celery
1 cup chopped yellow squash
1/2 cup chopped red onion
1/2 cup chopped red bell pepper

3 cups tarragon vinegar
1/2 cup vegetable oil
1/2 cup olive oil
1/2 cup sugar
3 garlic cloves, minced
2 teaspoons tarragon leaves
1 teaspoon prepared mustard
1 teaspoon salt

Combine the cauliflower, broccoli, zucchini, carrots, celery, squash, onion and bell pepper in a salad bowl. Combine the vinegar, vegetable oil, olive oil, sugar, garlic, tarragon, mustard and salt in a bowl and mix well. Pour over the cauliflower mixture and toss lightly to mix. Chill, covered, for 8 to 24 hours. Drain the vegetables just before serving.

Main Dishes

eef Stroganoff

1 (10-ounce) package frozen puff
    pastry shells
1 pound beef sirloin, cut into
    1 1/2-inch strips
1 1/2 cups sliced mushrooms

1 tablespoon vegetable oil
1 (12-ounce) jar beef gravy
1 (10-ounce) package frozen peas and
    pearl onions
1/4 cup sour cream

Bake the pastry shells using the package directions. Cook the beef and mushrooms in the vegetable oil in a skillet over medium heat until the beef is browned and the mushrooms are tender. Add the gravy and peas and pearl onions. Bring the mixture to a boil, stirring constantly. Reduce the heat to low. Simmer for 5 minutes. Stir in the sour cream. Cook until heated through. Spoon into the pastry shells. Garnish with parsley sprigs.

$\mathscr{S}$low-Cooked Pepper Steak

1 1/2 to 2 pounds beef round steak
2 tablespoons vegetable oil
1/4 cup soy sauce
1 cup chopped onion
1 garlic clove, minced
1 teaspoon sugar
1/2 teaspoon salt

1/4 teaspoon pepper
1/4 teaspoon ground ginger
4 tomatoes, cut into eighths, or
    1 (14-ounce) can diced tomatoes
2 large green bell peppers, cut into strips
1/2 cup cold water
1 tablespoon cornstarch

Cut the steak into 1×3-inch pieces. Cook in the vegetable oil in a skillet over medium-high heat until browned, stirring frequently. Remove to a slow cooker. Combine the soy sauce, onion, garlic, sugar, salt, pepper and ginger in a small bowl and mix well. Pour over the steak. Cook, covered, on Low for 5 to 6 hours or until the steak is tender. Stir in the tomatoes and bell peppers. Cook for 1 hour longer. Stir the water and cornstarch together in a small bowl to make a paste. Stir into the liquid in the slow cooker. Cook on High until thickened, stirring frequently. Serve over hot cooked noodles or rice.

Country-Fried Steak

2 pounds thick-cut round steak
1/2 cup flour
1 teaspoon salt
Pepper to taste

2 tablespoons shortening
1 small onion, chopped
1 1/2 cups boiling water
Dash of Worcestershire sauce (optional)

Cut the steak into 4 equal serving pieces. Pound with a meat mallet to tenderize. Coat the steaks with a mixture of the flour, salt and pepper, shaking off any excess. Brown the steaks on both sides in the shortening in a skillet. Add the onion, boiling water and Worcestershire sauce. Reduce the heat to low. Simmer for 1 hour, stirring in additional water if necessary to make gravy. Serve with hot cooked rice.

Beef Stew

1 1/2 pounds beef stew meat
3 tablespoons flour
2 tablespoons vegetable oil
1 cup water
1 cup chopped carrots
1 cup chopped peeled potatoes

1 cup chopped celery
1/2 cup chopped onion
1 garlic clove, minced
3 cups vegetable juice cocktail
1 teaspoon beef bouillon granules
1/2 teaspoon thyme

Coat the beef with the flour. Brown the beef in the vegetable oil in a Dutch oven over medium heat. Add the water. Simmer for 1 1/4 hours, stirring occasionally. Add the carrots, potatoes, celery, onion, garlic, vegetable juice cocktail, bouillon and thyme and stir to mix well. Simmer for 30 minutes longer or until vegetables are tender. May use pork instead of beef.

eat Loaf and Spaghetti

1 pound ground chuck
1 cup cooked rice
1 onion, chopped
3 tablespoons ketchup

Dash of Worcestershire sauce
1 (10-ounce) can tomato soup
1 soup can of water
1 (8-ounce) package spaghetti

Combine the ground chuck, rice, onion, ketchup and Worcestershire sauce in a bowl and mix well. Shape into a ball. Place in a baking dish. Bake at 350 degrees for 30 minutes or until cooked through. Heat the tomato soup and water in a small saucepan, stirring constantly. Cook the spaghetti using the package directions; drain. Arrange the spaghetti around the meat loaf. Pour the soup mixture over the spaghetti and meat loaf. Bake for 5 minutes longer.

tuffed Bell Peppers

6 large green bell peppers
1 pound ground chuck
1 onion, chopped
Soy sauce to taste
Worcestershire sauce to taste
Vegetable oil
2 cups steamed rice

1 1/2 teaspoons chili powder
1 1/2 teaspoons cinnamon
Lemon pepper to taste
Ketchup to taste
2 cups chopped fresh tomatoes
Salt and garlic salt to taste
Bread crumbs

Cut off the tops of the bell peppers; remove and discard the seeds and membranes. Place the bell peppers in boiling water to cover in a saucepan. Cook for 5 minutes; drain. Brown the ground chuck with the onion, soy sauce and Worcestershire sauce in a small amount of vegetable oil in a skillet, stirring until the ground chuck is crumbly; drain. Combine the ground chuck, rice, chili powder, cinnamon, lemon pepper, ketchup, tomatoes, salt and garlic salt in a large bowl and mix well.

Divide the mixture evenly among the prepared bell peppers. Top with bread crumbs. Stand the stuffed bell peppers in a baking pan just large enough to hold them upright. Pour a small amount of vegetable oil and water into the baking pan. Bake at 375 degrees for 35 minutes.

Beef and Rice Casserole

1 medium onion, chopped
1 green bell pepper, cut into thin rings
1 garlic clove, minced
2 tablespoons vegetable oil or shortening
1 pound ground beef

1 (16-ounce) can tomatoes
1 cup cooked rice
Salt to taste
Dash of pepper

Sauté the onion, bell pepper and garlic in the vegetable oil in a skillet until light brown, stirring constantly. Add the ground beef. Cook, stirring until the ground beef is crumbly; drain. Add the tomatoes, rice, salt and pepper and mix well, adding a small amount of water if needed to make of the desired consistency. Spoon into a baking dish. Bake at 300 degrees for 45 minutes. May cool and freeze this dish, covered, for future use. Thaw overnight in the refrigerator and bake as directed above.

Beef and Noodle Casserole

1 (8-ounce) package medium-wide egg
   noodles
1 1/2 pounds ground beef
1 large onion, chopped
Shortening

1 (8-ounce) can tomato sauce
1 (10-ounce) can cream of mushroom
   soup
8 ounces grated cheese
Salt and pepper to taste

Cook the egg noodles using the package directions; drain. Let stand to cool. Brown the ground beef with the onion in a small amount of shortening in a large skillet, stirring until the ground beef is crumbly; drain. Add the egg noodles, tomato sauce, soup and 3/4 of the cheese and stir until well mixed. Season with salt and pepper. Spoon the mixture into a baking dish. Sprinkle with the remaining cheese. Bake at 350 degrees for 30 minutes.

Apple Mushroom Pork Tenderloin

2 (12-ounce) boneless pork tenderloins,
   trimmed
3/4 cup flour
1/2 teaspoon salt
1/4 teaspoon pepper

1 garlic clove, minced
1 cup sliced fresh mushrooms
3/4 cup frozen apple juice concentrate,
   thawed, undiluted

Cut each pork tenderloin crosswise into 6 equal medallions. Pound the medallions 1/4 inch thick between sheets of heavy-duty plastic wrap. Mix the flour, salt and pepper together in a bowl. Dip the pork in the flour mixture to coat. Spray a nonstick skillet with nonstick cooking spray. Brown the pork in the skillet over medium heat. Remove from the skillet. Add the garlic and mushrooms to the skillet. Cook for 30 seconds, stirring constantly. Add the apple juice concentrate and the pork. Simmer for 3 minutes or until cooked through. May substitute 6 boneless skinless chicken breasts for the pork tenderloins.

Cranberry Pork Roast

1 (2 1/2- to 3-pound) boneless rolled pork
   loin roast
1 (16-ounce) can whole cranberry sauce,
   mashed
1/2 cup sugar
1/2 cup cranberry juice cocktail

1 teaspoon dry mustard
1/4 teaspoon ground cloves
2 tablespoons cornstarch
2 tablespoons cold water
Salt to taste

Place the roast in a slow cooker. Combine the cranberry sauce, sugar, cranberry juice cocktail, dry mustard and cloves in a medium bowl and mix well. Pour over the roast. Cook, covered, on Low for 6 to 8 hours or until the roast is tender. Remove the roast; keep warm. Skim the fat from the liquid. Add enough water to the liquid in the slow cooker to measure 2 cups. Pour into a saucepan. Bring to a boil over medium-high heat. Mix the cornstarch and cold water in a small bowl to make a paste. Stir into the mixture in the saucepan to make a gravy. Cook until thickened, stirring constantly. Stir in salt to taste. Slice the roast and serve with the gravy.

Honey Mustard Pork Tenderloin

2 (12-ounce) boneless pork tenderloins,
   trimmed
1/4 cup honey

2 tablespoons apple cider vinegar
1 tablespoon Dijon mustard
1/2 teaspoon paprika

Place the pork on a rack sprayed with nonstick cooking spray; set the rack in a broiler pan. Combine the honey, vinegar, Dijon mustard and paprika in a small bowl and mix well. Spoon 1/3 of the mixture over the pork. Bake at 350 degrees for 30 minutes or until a meat thermometer inserted into the thickest portion registers 160 degrees, basting occasionally with the remaining honey mixture. Slice the pork thinly to serve.

Sesame Pork Tenderloin

1/4 cup reduced-sodium soy sauce
1/4 cup orange juice
2 tablespoons honey
1 tablespoon finely chopped fresh
   gingerroot
1 garlic clove, minced
2 (12-ounce) boneless pork tenderloins,
   trimmed

4 1/2 teaspoons toasted sesame seeds
1/4 cup Burgundy or other dry red wine
1/4 cup ready-to-serve reduced-sodium
   nonfat chicken broth
2 teaspoons cornstarch
2 tablespoons water

Combine the soy sauce, orange juice, honey, gingerroot and garlic in a shallow dish and mix well. Add the pork, turning to coat. Chill, covered, for 8 hours, turning occasionally. Drain the pork, reserving the marinade. Place the pork in a roasting pan. Sprinkle with the sesame seeds. Bake at 350 degrees for 30 minutes or until a meat thermometer inserted into the thickest portion registers 160 degrees. Let stand for 15 minutes before slicing. Slice and keep warm.

Combine the reserved marinade, wine and broth in a saucepan. Bring to a boil, stirring constantly. Reduce the heat to low. Simmer for 5 minutes. Strain the sauce if desired. Combine the cornstarch and water in a small bowl. Stir into the sauce. Bring to a boil. Boil for 1 minute or until thickened, stirring constantly. Serve with the sliced pork.

Barbecued Pork Chops

8 lean pork chops
Shortening
1 cup water
1/2 cup ketchup

1/3 cup vinegar
1 teaspoon each salt and celery seeds
1/2 teaspoon nutmeg
1 bay leaf

Brown the pork chops in a small amount of shortening in a skillet. Arrange the pork chops in a baking dish. Combine the water, ketchup, vinegar, salt, celery seeds, nutmeg and bay leaf in a bowl and mix well. Pour over the pork chops. Bake, covered, at 325 degrees for 1 1/2 hours. Remove and discard the bay leaf before serving.

Barbecued Babyback Ribs

4 pounds babyback ribs
1 onion, cut into quarters
4 whole cloves
2 peppercorns
2 teaspoons salt
2 cups beer
1/2 cup honey

2/3 cup each soy sauce and ketchup
1 teaspoon each dry mustard, paprika
   and salt
1 cup red wine vinegar
1 cup orange juice
1/2 teaspoon hot red pepper sauce
1 garlic clove, crushed

Cut the babyback ribs into 4 equal portions containing 4 rib bones each or leave whole if desired. Combine the ribs, onion, cloves, peppercorns, 2 teaspoons salt and beer in a large stockpot and bring the mixture to a rolling boil. Reduce the heat to low. Simmer for 10 to 15 minutes. Drain the ribs, discarding the stock. Combine the honey, soy sauce, ketchup, dry mustard, paprika, 1 teaspoon salt, vinegar, orange juice, hot red pepper sauce and garlic in a medium saucepan and mix well. Bring to a boil over medium heat, stirring constantly. Reduce the heat to low. Simmer for 10 minutes. Pour the sauce into a large shallow dish. Marinate the ribs in the sauce for 8 to 10 hours or overnight.

Remove the ribs, reserving the sauce. Place the ribs on a hot grill, watching closely to prevent burning. Grill for 10 to 20 minutes or until fork-tender, turning frequently and basting with the sauce. For country-style or spareribs, cut ribs into individual portions and simmer in the beer stock for 20 minutes. Grill for 15 to 20 minutes or until fork-tender.

Country Ham with Red-Eye Gravy

4 (1/2-inch-thick) slices genuine
   country-cured ham
1 1/2 cups boiling water

1/4 cup strong brewed coffee
1 tablespoon brown sugar

Soak the ham slices in the water for a few minutes; drain and pat dry with paper towels. Remove and discard the hard black rind. Fry the ham slices in an ungreased heavy iron skillet over medium-high heat for 5 to 7 minutes on each side or until brown; do not burn. Remove to a platter, reserving 3 tablespoons of the drippings in the pan. Heat the drippings until smoking. Add the boiling water, coffee and brown sugar and bring to a boil, stirring constantly and scraping any browned bits from the bottom of the pan. Serve over hot biscuits or grits with the ham.

Brunswick Stew

1 (3-pound) pork roast
1 (2 1/2-pound) chicken
Salt and black pepper to taste
2 (15-ounce) cans tomatoes
3 large potatoes, peeled, cut into quarters

2 large onions, cut into quarters
2 (17-ounce) cans cream-style corn
1 (8-ounce) can tomato sauce
Cayenne pepper to taste

Place the pork roast and chicken in separate stockpots with water to cover. Bring each to a boil. Add salt and pepper. Cook the roast and the chicken until done. Remove the roast, discarding the stock. Remove the chicken, reserving the stock. Place the meat in a large food processor, discarding all bones and skin. Process until the meat is chopped; set aside.

Combine the undrained tomatoes, potatoes and onions in the food processor. Pulse until the vegetables are chopped. Combine the chopped vegetables and meat in a large pot and stir to mix. Add the corn, tomato sauce and cayenne pepper and mix well. Cook over low heat until the vegetables are tender, adding enough reserved chicken stock to make of the desired consistency.

Mother's Finest Southern Fried Chicken

1 (2- to 2^1/2-pound) chicken, cut into
   pieces, or 4 chicken breasts
1 teaspoon salt
1 teaspoon pepper
1 to 2 cups buttermilk
1 cup (or more) self-rising flour

2 cups vegetable oil
^{1}/2 cup (1 stick) margarine
3 tablespoons all-purpose flour
1 cup milk
1^1/2 to 2 cups water
Salt and pepper to taste

Sprinkle the chicken with 1 teaspoon salt and 1 teaspoon pepper. Dip in the buttermilk. Place the self-rising flour in a large sealable plastic bag. Place 3 or 4 chicken pieces at a time into the bag and seal the bag. Shake to coat the chicken. Heat the vegetable oil and margarine in a large deep cast-iron skillet to 350 degrees or until very hot but not smoking. Add 4 pieces of the coated chicken to the skillet. Fry until cooked through and evenly golden brown, turning just once using tongs. Drain on paper towels; keep warm. Repeat with the remaining chicken pieces until all are cooked. Drain all but ^{1}/4 cup drippings from the skillet. Stir in the all-purpose flour and salt and pepper to taste. Cook until bubbly. Add the milk and 1^1/2 cups of the water. Cook until thickened and bubbly, stirring constantly. Cook for 1 minute longer. Add remaining water, if necessary, for the desired consistency. Serve with the fried chicken.

Chicken with Tangy Apricot Glaze

8 pounds chicken pieces, skinned
1 envelope onion soup mix
1 (13-ounce) jar apricot preserves

1 (8-ounce) bottle Russian or spicy sweet
   French salad dressing

Place the chicken pieces in a large lightly greased roasting pan. Combine the soup mix, apricot preserves and salad dressing in a bowl and mix well. Spread over the chicken. Bake at 300 degrees for 2 hours or until cooked through.

Chicken Parmesan

1/4 cup fine bread crumbs
1/4 cup grated Parmesan cheese
1/4 teaspoon oregano
Dash of pepper
Dash of garlic powder

2 pounds chicken breasts or other pieces
1 (10-ounce) can cream of chicken or
  cream of mushroom soup
1/2 cup milk
Paprika

Mix the bread crumbs, half the Parmesan cheese, oregano, pepper and garlic powder in a shallow dish. Dip the chicken in the mixture to coat. Arrange in a greased 8×12-inch baking dish. Bake at 325 degrees for 20 minutes. Turn the chicken. Bake for 20 minutes longer. Combine the soup and milk in a bowl and mix well. Pour over the chicken. Sprinkle with the paprika and remaining cheese. Bake for 20 minutes longer or until the chicken is tender and cooked through.

Chicken and Mushrooms

2 tablespoons soy sauce
1 teaspoon finely chopped fresh
  gingerroot, or 1/4 teaspoon ground
  ginger
1/2 teaspoon sugar
1 teaspoon salt
1/8 teaspoon pepper
4 whole chicken breasts, cut into halves

1/4 cup vegetable oil
2 garlic cloves, finely chopped
2 (4-ounce) cans mushroom stems and
  pieces, drained
1 onion, thinly sliced, separated into rings
1 green bell pepper, seeded, sliced into
  rings

Mix the soy sauce, gingerroot, sugar, salt and pepper together in a shallow dish. Add 1 chicken breast at a time, rubbing the mixture over each piece to coat. Heat the vegetable oil in a large skillet over medium heat. Add the garlic and cook for 5 minutes or until light golden brown, stirring constantly. Add the chicken and cook, covered, over low heat for 35 minutes. Remove the cover and turn the chicken. Add the mushrooms, onion and bell pepper and cook, uncovered, for 10 minutes longer or until the chicken can be easily pierced with the tines of a fork.

aked Chicken Supreme

2 cups sour cream
$1/4$ cup lemon juice
4 teaspoons Worcestershire sauce
4 teaspoons celery salt
4 teaspoons garlic salt
2 teaspoons paprika

$1/2$ teaspoon pepper
6 whole chicken breasts, halved
$1^3/4$ cups dried bread crumbs
$1/2$ cup (1 stick) butter or margarine
$1/2$ cup shortening

Combine the sour cream, lemon juice, Worcestershire sauce, celery salt, garlic salt, paprika and pepper in a large bowl. Arrange the chicken in a single layer in a shallow pan. Pour the sour cream mixture over the chicken, coating each piece well. Chill, covered, for 8 to 10 hours.

Remove the chicken from the sour cream mixture. Coat with the bread crumbs. Arrange in a single layer in a 9×13-inch baking pan. Melt the butter and shortening in a saucepan over medium heat and mix well. Spoon half the butter mixture over the chicken.

Bake at 350 degrees for 45 minutes. Spoon the remaining butter mixture over the chicken. Bake for 10 to 15 minutes longer or until the chicken is cooked through and brown.

asil Grilled Chicken

1/2 cup (1 stick) butter or margarine,
   softened
2 tablespoons finely chopped fresh basil
1 tablespoon grated Parmesan cheese
1/4 teaspoon garlic powder
1/8 teaspoon salt

1/8 teaspoon pepper
3/4 teaspoon coarsely ground pepper
4 skinless chicken breast halves
5 1/3 tablespoons butter or margarine,
   melted
1/4 cup chopped fresh basil

For the basil butter, combine the softened butter, 2 tablespoons basil, Parmesan cheese, garlic powder, salt and pepper in a small mixing bowl. Beat at low speed until smooth. Remove to a small serving bowl. Chill, covered, until serving time.

For the chicken, press the coarsely ground pepper into the meaty sides of the chicken. Combine the melted butter and 1/4 cup basil in a small bowl and mix well. Brush the chicken lightly with some of the melted butter mixture, reserving the remaining butter mixture. Grill the chicken over medium coals for 8 to 10 minutes per side, basting frequently with the reserved melted butter mixture. Remove the chicken to a serving platter. Garnish with fresh basil sprigs. Serve with the chilled basil butter.

Company Chicken Cordon Bleu

8 boneless skinless chicken breast halves
1/4 teaspoon salt
1/4 teaspoon white pepper
1 cup milk
2 eggs, beaten
4 (1-ounce) slices cooked ham,
 cut into halves

4 (1-ounce) slices Swiss cheese,
 cut into halves
1/3 cup flour
1 1/3 cups fine dry bread crumbs
Vegetable oil for frying
Mushroom Sauce (optional)

Flatten each piece of chicken between 2 sheets of waxed paper to 1/4 inch thickness using a meat mallet or rolling pin. Sprinkle with the salt and white pepper. Combine the milk and eggs in a small bowl and mix well. Brush both sides of the chicken with the milk mixture. Place a piece of ham and a piece of Swiss cheese on each piece of chicken. Brush the top of the cheese with milk mixture. Fold ends of chicken over the ham and cheese. Roll as for a jelly roll, beginning at one long side. Secure with wooden picks. Coat chicken with flour and dip in remaining milk mixture. Coat with bread crumbs. Chill, covered, for 1 hour. Pour enough vegetable oil to measure 1/2 inch into a heavy skillet. Cook chicken in hot oil over medium heat for 20 minutes or until cooked through and golden brown, turning frequently; drain well. Serve with Mushroom Sauce.

Mushroom Sauce

1 (10-ounce) can cream of mushroom
 soup
1 cup sour cream

1 (4-ounce) can sliced mushrooms,
 drained
1/3 cup dry sherry

Combine the soup, sour cream, mushrooms and sherry in a saucepan. Cook over medium heat until heated through, stirring occasionally.

hicken Breasts in Phyllo

1 cup mayonnaise or mayonnaise-type
  salad dressing
2/3 cup chopped green onions
3¹/2 tablespoons fresh lemon juice
1 small garlic clove, minced
3/4 teaspoon tarragon

8 boneless skinless chicken breasts
1/4 teaspoon salt
1/8 teaspoon pepper
16 sheets frozen phyllo dough, thawed
3¹/2 tablespoons grated Parmesan cheese

Combine the mayonnaise, green onions, lemon juice, garlic and tarragon in a small bowl and mix well. Sprinkle the chicken with the salt and pepper. Place 1 sheet of phyllo dough on a sheet of plastic wrap and spray evenly with butter-flavor nonstick cooking spray. Place another sheet of phyllo dough on top and spray with butter-flavor nonstick cooking spray.

Spread 3 tablespoons of the mayonnaise mixture over both sides of 1 chicken breast. Place chicken breast diagonally in one corner of the stacked phyllo sheets. Fold the corner over the chicken breast, then fold the sides over and roll as for a jelly roll, completely enclosing the chicken breast in the dough. Place seam side down in an ungreased 10×15-inch baking pan.

Repeat with the remaining chicken breasts and phyllo dough sheets until all are used. Spray the tops of the dough packets with butter-flavor nonstick cooking spray. Sprinkle evenly with the Parmesan cheese. Bake at 350 degrees for 40 to 45 minutes or until the chicken is cooked through. Serve immediately.

ld-Fashioned Chicken and Dumplings

1 (2¹/2- to 3-pound) chicken
8 cups water
1 teaspoon salt
¹/2 teaspoon pepper
2 cups flour

¹/2 teaspoon baking soda
¹/2 teaspoon salt
3 tablespoons shortening
³/4 cup buttermilk

Place the chicken in a Dutch oven. Add the water and 1 teaspoon salt and bring to a boil. Reduce the heat and simmer, covered, for 1 hour or until chicken is tender. Remove the chicken, reserving the stock. Let the chicken stand to cool slightly. Remove the chicken from the bones and cut into bite-size pieces; set aside.

Bring the stock to a boil. Stir in the pepper. Combine the flour, baking soda and ¹/2 teaspoon salt in a medium bowl. Cut in the shortening until the mixture resembles coarse meal. Add the buttermilk, stirring with a fork until the dry ingredients are moistened. Knead lightly 4 or 5 times on a well-floured surface. Pat the dough ¹/4 inch thick. Pinch off 1¹/2-inch pieces and drop into the boiling stock. Reduce the heat to medium-low. Cook the dumplings for 8 to 10 minutes or until done to taste. Stir in the chicken and serve.

For rolled dumplings, roll the dough ¹/4 inch thick on a lightly floured surface. Cut the dough into ¹/2x4-inch strips. Drop the dough 1 strip at a time into the boiling stock, stirring gently after each addition. Proceed as above.

Chicken Potpie

1 cooked chicken, boned, or 3 chicken
   breasts, cooked, boned
2 (9-ounce) cans Veg-All, partially
   drained
2 (10-ounce) cans cream of chicken soup

1 (10-ounce) can cream of celery soup
4 hard-cooked eggs, chopped
1 onion, finely chopped
2 to 3 cups strained chicken broth
1 (1-crust) pie pastry

Chop the chicken into bite-size pieces. Combine the chicken, Veg-All, soups, eggs and onion in a large bowl and mix well. Add enough of the chicken broth to make of the desired consistency, stirring until well mixed. Pour into a pie plate. Top with the pie pastry, tucking the edges under and fluting and cutting vents. Bake at 400 degrees for 25 to 30 minutes or until golden brown and bubbly. Cool slightly before serving. You may top the filling with a mixture of 3/4 cup mayonnaise, 1 cup flour and 1 cup milk instead of the pie pastry. Bake at 350 degrees until golden brown.

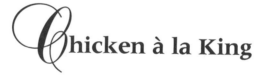

Chicken à la King

1 (10-ounce) package frozen puff pastry
   shells
1/2 cup chopped green bell pepper
2 tablespoons butter or margarine

1 (10-ounce) can cream of chicken soup
1/2 cup milk
2 cups chopped cooked chicken or turkey
1/4 cup chopped pimentos

Bake the pastry shells using the package directions; keep warm. Sauté the bell pepper in the butter in a skillet until tender. Add the soup, milk, chicken and pimentos and stir until well mixed. Heat to serving temperature, stirring occasionally. Spoon into the warm pastry shells and serve.

$\mathcal{P}$ineapple Chicken Stir-Fry

1½ pounds boneless chicken fillets,
   cut into small pieces
2 tablespoons olive oil
2 large onions, chopped
Garlic salt to taste
Pepper to taste
6 cups chopped broccoli

2 cups chopped mushrooms
1 cup chopped carrots
2 cups chopped pineapple
2 to 3 tablespoons cornstarch
5 to 6 tablespoons soy sauce
½ cup pineapple juice
6 cups cooked rice

Brown the chicken in the olive oil in a large skillet over medium-high heat. Stir in the onions and season with the garlic salt and pepper to taste. Layer the broccoli, mushrooms, carrots and pineapple over the top; do not stir. Add 2 to 3 tablespoons water and allow the vegetables to steam over low heat for 10 to 12 minutes or until vegetables are bright in color and tender-crisp. Combine the cornstarch, soy sauce and pineapple juice in a small bowl and mix well. Pour over the vegetables and cook for 2 to 5 minutes longer or until the sauce thickens. Stir all the ingredients together. Serve over the rice.

$\mathcal{C}$hicken Delight

4 or 5 chicken breasts
½ cup chopped celery
¼ cup mayonnaise
1 cup water chestnuts, chopped
1 (10-ounce) can cream of mushroom
   soup

½ cup (1 stick) margarine
½ (8-ounce) package herb-seasoned
   stuffing mix

Combine the chicken and celery in a large pot with water to cover. Bring to a boil. Cook until the chicken is cooked through. Remove the chicken and allow to cool slightly. Strain and reserve ½ cup of the cooking liquid. Remove the chicken from the bones and chop into small pieces. Combine with the mayonnaise, water chestnuts, soup and reserved liquid in a bowl and mix well. Spoon into a 9-inch square baking dish. Melt the butter in a medium skillet and add the stuffing mix, stirring to combine. Spread over the top of the chicken mixture. Bake at 350 degrees for 30 minutes or until the top is brown. Serve over hot cooked rice.

Chicken and Rice Casserole

3 cups coarsely chopped cooked chicken
   breasts
3 cups cooked rice
2 tablespoons chopped onion
1 (8-ounce) can sliced water chestnuts,
   drained

1 cup chopped celery
2 (10-ounce) cans cream of chicken soup
1 cup sour cream
1/2 cup sliced almonds
2 cups crushed cornflakes
1/4 cup (1/2 stick) margarine, melted

Combine the chicken, rice, onion, water chestnuts, celery, soup, sour cream and almonds in a large bowl and stir gently until well mixed. Spoon into a greased casserole and sprinkle evenly with the cornflakes. Drizzle with the margarine. Bake at 350 degrees for 45 minutes. You may prepare this 1 day ahead and refrigerate overnight before baking.

Chicken and Wild Rice Casserole

2 cups long grain and wild rice mix
1 cup chopped onion
1 cup (2 sticks) butter
1/2 cup flour
2 (4-ounce) cans chopped mushrooms
3 (10-ounce) cans (or more) chicken
   broth

3 cups light cream
4 cups chopped cooked chicken
1 cup slivered almonds, toasted
1/4 cup chopped fresh parsley, or
   1 teaspoon dried parsley
1 tablespoon salt
1/2 teaspoon pepper

Prepare the rice using the package directions. Sauté the onion in the butter in a large sauté pan until tender. Remove from the heat and stir in the flour. Drain the mushrooms, reserving the liquid. Combine the reserved liquid with enough chicken broth to measure 4 cups. Stir into the flour mixture gradually. Return to the heat. Add the cream. Cook until thickened, stirring constantly. Add the rice, mushrooms, chicken, almonds, parsley, salt and pepper and stir until well mixed. Spoon into a baking dish. Bake at 350 degrees for 30 to 45 minutes or until heated through. You may prepare this casserole 1 day ahead and refrigerate overnight before baking.

Chicken Casserole

4 boneless chicken breasts, cooked,
   chopped
1 cup mayonnaise
1 cup chopped celery

1 (10-ounce) can cream of chicken soup
1/2 cup slivered almonds
1/2 cup (1 stick) margarine, melted
1 sleeve butter crackers, crushed

Combine the chicken, mayonnaise, celery, soup and almonds in a bowl and mix well. Spoon into a baking dish. Top evenly with a mixture of the margarine and crushed crackers. Bake at 350 degrees for 30 minutes.

Chicken Florentine

3 tablespoons butter
3 tablespoons flour
1 cup milk
1/2 cup cream
Salt and pepper to taste
1/4 teaspoon nutmeg

2 (10-ounce) packages frozen spinach,
   cooked, drained
12 slices cooked chicken
4 to 5 tablespoons grated Parmesan
   cheese

Melt the butter in a saucepan over medium heat. Blend in the flour. Add the milk and cream gradually, stirring constantly. Cook over low heat until smooth and thickened, stirring constantly. Season with salt, pepper and nutmeg. Combine the spinach and 1/2 cup of the cream sauce in a saucepan. Cook over low heat until heated through. Spoon into a baking dish. Arrange the chicken slices over the top. Stir 3 tablespoons of the Parmesan cheese into the remaining cream sauce and pour over the chicken. Sprinkle evenly with the remaining cheese. Broil until light brown.

Hot Chicken Salad Casserole

2 cups chopped cooked chicken
2 cups chopped celery
1 tablespoon chopped onion
1 cup mayonnaise

1/2 cup sliced almonds
1 tablespoon lemon juice
1 cup shredded American cheese
1 cup crushed potato chips

Combine the chicken, celery, onion, mayonnaise, almonds and lemon juice in a bowl and stir gently until well mixed. Spoon into a baking dish. Sprinkle the cheese and crushed potato chips over the top. Bake at 350 degrees for 30 minutes or until the cheese is melted. May substitute turkey for the chicken.

Crab Casserole

1 cup sliced fresh or canned mushrooms
1 tablespoon chopped chives
1 tablespoon chopped onion
1/4 cup (1/2 stick) butter
1/3 cup flour
1/2 cup cream
2 cups milk
3 egg yolks, beaten

3 tablespoons sherry
2 tablespoons chopped parsley
1 1/2 teaspoons prepared mustard
1 pound crab meat, cooked
Salt and pepper to taste
Shredded Swiss cheese
Bread crumbs

Sauté the mushrooms, chives and onion in the butter in a large sauté pan over medium-high heat, stirring constantly. Add the flour and stir to combine. Add the cream and milk gradually, stirring constantly. Cook until thickened, stirring constantly. Remove from the heat.

Add the egg yolks to the cream mixture gradually, stirring constantly. Stir in the sherry, parsley, mustard, crab meat and salt and pepper. Spoon into a casserole and sprinkle with cheese and bread crumbs. Broil for 5 minutes. Serve over hot cooked rice or pasta.

Crab and Shrimp Shells

1 (10-ounce) package frozen puff pastry
   shells
2 (10-ounce) cans cream of shrimp soup
1 (6-ounce) can crab meat, drained
8 ounces peeled cooked shrimp

1 (2-ounce) jar sliced pimentos, drained
1 (8-ounce) can green peas, drained
1 cup sour cream
4 ounces grated Parmesan cheese

Bake the pastry shells using the package directions. Combine the next 6 ingredients in a large bowl and mix well. Spoon into a greased 8×11-inch baking dish. Sprinkle with the Parmesan cheese. Bake at 350 degrees for 30 minutes. Serve in the baked pastry shells.

Shrimp and Artichoke Bake

2 (14-ounce) cans artichoke hearts
1/4 cup (1/2 stick) butter
2 medium onions, chopped
1 pound mushrooms, sliced
1 teaspoon lemon pepper
1 pound peeled cooked shrimp
1/4 cup (1/2 stick) butter

5 tablespoons flour
3/4 cup heavy cream
1/2 cup dry sherry
1/2 teaspoon each salt, pepper and paprika
1 tablespoon Worcestershire sauce
1/4 cup (1/2 stick) butter, melted
1 (16-ounce) package croutons

For the shrimp and artichokes, drain the artichoke hearts, reserving 3/4 cup of the liquid. Cut the artichokes into quarters. Spray a large sauté pan with nonstick cooking spray. Melt 1/4 cup butter in the pan. Add the onions and sauté until translucent. Add the mushrooms and sauté until tender. Place the mixture in a 7×11-inch glass baking dish. Sprinkle with the lemon pepper. Arrange the shrimp over the top and scatter the artichokes over the shrimp.

For the sauce, melt 1/4 cup butter in a medium saucepan over medium heat. Stir in the flour. Cook for 1 minute, stirring constantly. Combine the reserved artichoke liquid, heavy cream and sherry in a medium bowl and mix well. Pour into the flour mixture gradually, stirring constantly. Stir in the salt, pepper, paprika and Worcestershire sauce. Bring to a boil, stirring constantly. Pour over the artichokes and shrimp.

For the topping, combine 1/4 cup butter and croutons in a medium bowl and mix until moistened. Sprinkle over the sauce. Bake, covered with foil, at 350 degrees for 35 minutes.

Quiche

3 eggs, beaten
1 cup milk
Salt and pepper to taste
Dash of nutmeg
4 ounces shredded Swiss cheese

2 tablespoons flour
Sautéed grated onions
Sliced fresh mushrooms (optional)
1 unbaked (9-inch) pie shell

Combine the eggs, milk, salt, pepper, nutmeg, Swiss cheese, flour, onions and mushrooms in a large bowl and stir gently until well mixed. Pour into the pie shell. Bake at 350 degrees for 45 minutes or until set. You may add or substitute items of choice for this recipe such as 1 package frozen spinach, cooked, 6 ounces crab meat, or vegetables of choice.

Egg Soufflé

3 slices white bread, torn into pieces
3 eggs, beaten
1 1/2 cups milk
8 ounces shredded Cheddar cheese

1 teaspoon dry mustard
1 teaspoon salt
1/8 teaspoon pepper

Place the bread pieces in a soufflé dish. Combine the eggs, milk, Cheddar cheese, mustard, salt and pepper in a bowl and mix well. Pour over the bread. Chill, covered, overnight. Bake at 350 degrees for 45 minutes or until puffy and golden brown. You may add crumbled browned sausage to the batter before baking if desired.

Barbecue Sauce

1/4 cup chopped onion
1 tablespoon butter or margarine
2 tablespoons vinegar
1 tablespoon Worcestershire sauce
1/4 cup lemon juice
2 tablespoons brown sugar

1/2 teaspoon garlic salt
1/4 teaspoon paprika
1 (10-ounce) can tomato soup
1 soup can of water
1 thin slice fresh lemon

Sauté the onion in the butter in a medium saucepan until tender; do not brown. Add the vinegar, Worcestershire sauce, lemon juice, brown sugar, garlic salt, paprika, tomato soup, water and lemon slice and mix well. Simmer for 15 minutes, stirring occasionally. Use to marinate and baste pork chops for grilling.

Sweet-and-Sour Sauce

1 (20-ounce) can pineapple chunks
2 tablespoons cornstarch
1/2 teaspoon salt
3/4 cup sugar
2 teaspoons Worcestershire sauce

5 dashes of Tabasco sauce
1/2 cup vinegar
1/2 cup ketchup
2 green bell peppers, cut into large pieces
2 onions, cut into large pieces

Drain the pineapple, reserving the liquid. Add enough water to the liquid to measure 3/4 cup. Combine with the cornstarch, salt, sugar, Worcestershire sauce, Tabasco sauce, vinegar and ketchup in a large saucepan and mix well. Cook over low heat until thickened, stirring occasionally. Add the bell peppers and onions. Simmer for 2 minutes longer. Add the pineapple. Cook for 30 seconds. Use with meatballs at weddings and parties, or add chicken nuggets or pork pieces and serve over rice for an entrée.

Side
Dishes

Southern Corn Bread Dressing

6 cups crumbled corn bread
4 1/2 cups dry white bread crumbs
8 cups chicken or turkey broth
1 cup (2 sticks) butter, melted
1 cup finely chopped onion
1 cup finely chopped celery

2 tablespoons sage
2 tablespoons sugar
1 tablespoon salt
2 teaspoons pepper
8 eggs, beaten

Combine the corn bread and white bread in a bowl and mix well. Stir in the broth, butter, onion, celery, sage, sugar, salt and pepper. Add eggs and mix well. Add additional broth if mixture appears dry. Spoon into a buttered baking dish. Bake at 400 degrees for 45 minutes or until golden brown.

Squash Dressing

1 beef bouillon cube
1 cup hot water
2 cups crumbled corn bread
2 slices white bread, crumbled
2 cups chopped cooked squash, drained
1 medium onion, chopped

1/2 cup (1 stick) margarine, melted
1/2 cup milk
2 eggs
1 teaspoon sage (optional)
Salt and pepper to taste

Dissolve the bouillon cube in the hot water in a large bowl. Add the corn bread, white bread, squash, onion, margarine, milk, eggs, sage, salt and pepper and mix well. Spoon into a baking dish. Bake at 350 degrees until set and brown.

acaroni and Cheese

8 ounces elbow macaroni
1/2 cup (1 stick) margarine
1/3 cup flour
1 teaspoon salt

1/4 teaspoon pepper
2 1/2 cups milk
2 cups shredded Velveeta cheese

Cook the macaroni using the package directions; drain. Melt the butter in a saucepan over low heat. Add the flour, salt and pepper and mix until smooth. Stir in the milk. Cook over medium-high heat until thickened and bubbly, stirring constantly. Remove from the heat. Stir in the Velveeta cheese. Place the cooked macaroni in a baking dish. Pour the cheese mixture over the macaroni. Bake at 350 degrees for 20 minutes.

Easy and Quick Wild Rice Casserole

2 tablespoons butter
1 (7-ounce) can mushroom stems and
   pieces, drained
1/2 cup wild rice

1/4 cup slivered almonds
1 tablespoon chopped onion
1 1/2 cups chicken broth

Melt the butter in a large skillet over low heat. Stir in the mushrooms, rice, almonds and onion. Cook for 20 minutes, stirring occasionally. Add the broth and mix well. Spoon into a 1-quart baking dish. Bake, covered, at 300 degrees for 2 hours or at 350 degrees for 1 hour.

ellow Rice Casserole

1 (10-ounce) can French onion soup
1 cup water
1 (7-ounce) can mushroom stems and
   pieces, drained

1 can water chestnuts, drained and
   chopped
1 (5-ounce) package yellow rice
1/2 cup (1 stick) butter, melted

Combine the soup, water, mushrooms, water chestnuts, rice and butter in a bowl and mix well. Spoon into a baking dish. Bake, covered, at 350 degrees for 1 hour.

risp Cucumber Pickles

2 gallons water
3 cups pickling lime
7 pounds cucumbers, sliced 1/4 inch thick
2 tablespoons pickling spices

2 quarts vinegar
9 cups sugar
1 teaspoon salt

Combine the water and lime in a crock and mix well. Add the cucumbers. Let stand, covered, for 24 hours, stirring occasionally. Remove the cucumbers; drain. Rinse and drain well. Combine the cucumbers and enough ice water to cover in a large container. Let stand, covered, for 4 hours, draining the cucumbers and replacing the ice water every hour. Remove the cucumbers from the water. Tie the pickling spices in cheesecloth. Combine the vinegar, sugar and salt in a large container and mix well. Add the spice bag and cucumbers. Let stand, covered, overnight. Place the cucumber mixture in a saucepan. Bring to a boil over medium heat. Cook for 30 minutes, stirring occasionally. Pack the cucumbers and syrup into hot sterilized jars, leaving 1/2 inch headspace; seal with 2-piece lids. Process in a boiling water bath for 10 minutes.

each Pickles

1 tablespoon pickling spices
2 cups sugar
1 cup vinegar

1 cup water
18 to 24 peaches, peeled

Tie the pickling spices in cheesecloth. Combine the sugar, vinegar and water in a saucepan and mix well. Cook over low heat until syrup thickens, stirring constantly. Add the peaches a few at a time. Cook peaches just until tender. Pack the peaches and syrup in hot sterilized jars, leaving 1/2 inch headspace; seal with 2-piece lids. Process in a boiling water bath for 10 minutes.

pple Butter

15 medium tart cooking apples (about 4
  to 5 pounds)
1 1/2 quarts apple cider
3 cups sugar

1 teaspoon cinnamon
1 teaspoon allspice
1 teaspoon ground cloves
1/4 teaspoon nutmeg

Slice the unpeeled apples; do not remove the cores and seeds. Combine the apples and apple cider in a saucepan. Bring to a boil over medium-high heat. Boil for 15 minutes or until apples are tender, stirring occasionally. Press the apples through a sieve. Place the apple pulp in a saucepan. Bring to a boil over medium-low heat. Boil for 1 hour or until mixture begins to thicken, stirring occasionally. Stir in the cinnamon, allspice, cloves and nutmeg. Cook over low heat for 3 hours or until thickened, stirring frequently. Pour into hot sterilized jars, leaving 1/4 inch headspace; seal with 2-piece lids. Process in a boiling water bath for 10 minutes.

 **ig Preserves**

2 quarts fresh figs (about 4 pounds)   8 cups sugar

Layer the figs and sugar in several layers in a Dutch oven. Let stand, covered, for 8 hours. Cook over medium heat for 2 hours or until the syrup thickens and the figs are transparent. Pack the fig mixture into hot sterilized jars, leaving 1/2 inch headspace, removing any air bubbles; seal with 2-piece lids. Process in a boiling water bath for 15 minutes.

 **ear Preserves**

3 gallons sliced cooking pears   1 lemon, sliced
5 pounds sugar

Combine the pears and sugar in a Dutch oven. Let stand, covered, overnight. Add the lemon. Cook over medium heat for 2 hours or until the pears become amber in color and syrup thickens, stirring occasionally. Remove the lemon. Spoon into hot sterilized jars; seal with 2-piece lids. Process in a boiling water bath for 10 minutes.

Layered Vegetable Casserole

1 package frozen French-style green
  beans, thawed
1 package frozen baby lima beans,
  thawed
1 package frozen green peas, thawed
Salt and pepper to taste
2 green bell peppers, cut into thin strips
  and blanched

1/2 cup thinly sliced onion
1 cup whipping cream, whipped
1 cup mayonnaise
3/4 cup grated Parmesan cheese
3/4 cup shredded Cheddar cheese

Layer the green beans, lima beans and green peas in a buttered 2-quart baking dish, sprinkling each layer with salt and pepper. Layer with the bell peppers and onion. Combine the whipped cream, mayonnaise, Parmesan cheese, Cheddar cheese, salt and pepper in a bowl and mix well. Spread over the top of the vegetables. Chill, covered, until ready to bake. Bake at 325 degrees for 50 minutes or until brown and puffy.

Home-Style Baked Beans

2 (28-ounce) cans baked beans with
  tangy sauce, bacon and brown sugar
1 sweet onion, quartered
1 cup ketchup

1/2 to 3/4 cup prepared mustard
2 tablespoons light brown sugar
4 slices bacon

Combine the baked beans, onion, ketchup, mustard and brown sugar in a bowl and mix well. Spoon into a lightly greased 7×11-inch baking dish. Arrange bacon over the top. Bake at 400 degrees for 45 minutes. Broil 5 inches from heat source for 1 minute to brown the bacon, propping oven door partially open.

aked Beans

1 (31-ounce) can pork and beans
1 small can pork barbecue
1 medium onion, chopped

1 cup packed brown sugar
1 cup ketchup
2 teaspoons dry mustard

Combine the pork and beans, barbecue, onion, brown sugar, ketchup and dry mustard in a bowl and mix well. Spoon into a baking dish. Bake, covered, at 300 degrees for 3 to 4 hours, stirring occasionally.

reen Bean Bundles

2 cans whole green beans, drained
1 pound bacon
6 tablespoons butter
1 cup liquid brown sugar

Salt to taste
Dash of pepper
Dash of garlic salt

Roll 8 green beans in 1/2 slice of bacon; secure with wooden picks. Repeat procedure with remaining green beans and bacon. Arrange in an 11×13-inch baking dish. Melt the butter in a saucepan over medium heat. Stir in the brown sugar, salt, pepper and garlic salt. Pour over the green bean bundles. Bake, covered, at 350 degrees for 45 minutes. Bake, uncovered, for 15 minutes longer.

Seasoned Green Beans

4 cups snapped fresh flat green beans
1 small piece salt pork

2 tablespoons sugar
Salt to taste

Combine the beans, salt pork, sugar, salt and enough water to cover in a saucepan. Bring to a boil over medium-high heat. Reduce heat to medium-low. Boil until beans and salt pork are tender; drain. May use two 15¼-ounce cans Italian green beans instead of fresh green beans. Rinse and drain the canned green beans before proceeding with the recipe.

Lemon Broccoli

2 tablespoons grated lemon zest
¼ teaspoon salt
¼ teaspoon freshly ground pepper

1½ pounds broccoli
2 tablespoons lemon juice

Combine the lemon zest, salt and pepper in a bowl and mix well. Remove and discard the leaves and tough ends of the stalks from the broccoli. Cut the broccoli into spears. Place in a steamer basket over boiling water. Steam, covered, for 5 minutes or until tender-crisp. Arrange the broccoli on a serving plate. Sprinkle with the lemon zest mixture and lemon juice.

Broccoli Casserole

2 packages frozen chopped broccoli
1 (10-ounce) can cream of mushroom
 soup
1 cup shredded Cheddar cheese

3/4 cup mayonnaise
1 egg, beaten
1 tablespoon minced onion
Crushed butter crackers

Cook the broccoli using the package directions; drain. Combine the broccoli, soup, Cheddar cheese, mayonnaise, egg and onion in a bowl and mix well. Spoon into a baking dish. Sprinkle with cracker crumbs. Bake at 350 degrees for 30 minutes.

Broccoli Cauliflower Casserole

1 (10-ounce) package frozen chopped
 broccoli
1 (10-ounce) package frozen cauliflower
1 (10-ounce) can cream of mushroom
 soup

8 ounces shredded cheese
1 (10-ounce) can cream of celery soup
1 sleeve butter crackers, crushed
1/2 cup (1 stick) margarine, melted

Cook the broccoli and cauliflower separately using the package directions; drain. Layer the broccoli, mushroom soup, half the cheese, cauliflower, celery soup and remaining cheese in a baking dish. Combine the crackers and margarine in a bowl and mix well. Sprinkle over the vegetable mixture. Bake at 350 degrees for 30 minutes.

Green Broccoli Ring and Beets

2 packages frozen chopped broccoli
2 tablespoons butter
2 tablespoons flour
1/2 teaspoon salt
1 cup milk

3/4 cup mayonnaise
3 eggs, beaten
1 cup pickled beets
1 tablespoon vinegar

Cook the broccoli using the package directions; drain. Mash the broccoli thoroughly. Melt the butter in a saucepan over medium heat. Add the flour and salt and stir until smooth. Stir in the milk. Cook until thickened, stirring constantly. Spoon into a greased ring mold. Place in a hot water bath. Bake at 350 degrees for 35 to 40 minutes or until set. Unmold onto a serving plate. Combine the undrained pickled beets and vinegar in a saucepan. Cook over medium heat until heated through; drain. Spoon the beets into the center of the broccoli ring.

Baked Cabbage

3 cups shredded cabbage
3/4 cup cream
2 eggs, beaten
1 tablespoon sugar

1/2 teaspoon salt
Shredded Cheddar cheese
Bread crumbs
Butter

Place the cabbage in an 8×8-inch baking dish. Combine the cream, eggs, sugar and salt in a bowl and mix well. Pour over the cabbage. Sprinkle the top with Cheddar cheese and bread crumbs. Dot with butter. Bake at 325 degrees for 40 to 45 minutes.

Marinated Carrots

2 pounds carrots
1 green bell pepper, chopped
1 onion, thinly sliced
1 (10-ounce) can cream of tomato soup
3/4 cup sugar
3/4 cup vinegar

1/2 cup corn oil
1 teaspoon salt
1 teaspoon Worcestershire sauce
1 teaspoon dry mustard
1/4 teaspoon pepper

Cut the carrots into thin strips or slices. Combine the carrots and enough water to cover in a saucepan. Cook over medium-high heat just until tender; drain. Combine the carrots, bell pepper and onion in a bowl. Combine the soup, sugar, vinegar, corn oil, salt, Worcestershire sauce, dry mustard and pepper in a saucepan and mix well. Bring to a boil over medium-high heat. Cook for 10 minutes, stirring frequently. Pour over the carrot mixture. Let stand to cool. Chill, covered, overnight or for up to 3 weeks.

Southern-Style Creamed Corn

6 medium ears of Silver Queen corn
1/4 cup (1/2 stick) butter or margarine
1/4 cup water
1/2 cup milk

2 teaspoons flour or cornstarch
1/2 teaspoon salt
1/4 teaspoon white pepper

Cut the corn from the cobs, scraping the cobs well to remove all the liquid. Combine the corn, butter and water in a saucepan. Cook over medium heat for 10 minutes or until the corn is tender. Meanwhile, combine the milk, flour, salt and white pepper in a bowl and beat with a wire whip until blended. Stir into the corn mixture. Cook for 3 minutes or until thickened and bubbly, stirring frequently. May substitute 2 packages frozen Shoe Peg corn for the fresh corn. Pulse 2 or 3 times in a food processor before proceeding with the recipe.

Fried Okra

1 pound okra
2 cups buttermilk
1 1/2 cups self-rising cornmeal
1/2 cup self-rising flour

1 teaspoon salt
Vegetable oil
1/4 cup bacon drippings (optional)

Cut off and discard the tips and stem ends of the okra. Cut the okra into 1/2-inch-thick slices. Combine the okra and buttermilk in a bowl and mix well. Chill, covered, for 45 minutes. Combine the cornmeal, flour and salt in a bowl and mix well. Drain the okra. Coat the okra in batches in the cornmeal mixture. Pour the oil to a depth of 2 inches into a Dutch oven or cast-iron skillet; add the bacon drippings. Heat to 375 degrees. Fry the okra in batches in the hot oil for 4 minutes or until golden; drain on paper towels.

Honey-Baked Georgia Sweet Onions

6 medium Georgia sweet onions
1 1/2 cups tomato juice
1 1/2 cups water

3 tablespoons butter, melted
6 teaspoons honey

Peel and trim the onions. Cut the onions into halves. Arrange in a buttered baking dish. Combine the tomato juice, water, butter and honey in a bowl and mix well. Pour over the onions. Bake at 325 degrees for 1 hour or until tender.

Pineapple Casserole

1 (20-ounce) can pineapple chunks
3 tablespoons flour
3 tablespoons sugar

1¼ cups shredded Cheddar cheese
1½ cups crushed butter crackers
3 tablespoons butter, melted

Drain the pineapple, reserving 3 tablespoons of the juice. Place the pineapple in a 1½-quart baking dish. Combine the flour and sugar in a bowl and mix well. Sprinkle over the pineapple. Drizzle the reserved juice over the flour mixture. Sprinkle with the Cheddar cheese. Combine the crackers and butter in a bowl and mix well. Sprinkle over the cheese. Bake, covered, at 350 degrees for 15 minutes. Bake, uncovered, for 10 minutes longer.

Hash Brown Potato Casserole

1 (2-pound) package frozen hash brown
   potatoes
8 ounces shredded Cheddar cheese
10 to 12 ounces sour cream
1 (10-ounce) can cream of chicken soup

½ cup chopped green onions
½ cup (1 stick) margarine, melted
1 teaspoon salt
1 teaspoon pepper

Thaw the potatoes for 30 minutes. Reserve 3 tablespoons of the Cheddar cheese. Combine the potatoes, sour cream, soup, remaining Cheddar cheese, green onions, margarine, salt and pepper in a bowl and mix well. Spoon into a 9×13-inch baking dish. Bake at 350 degrees for 55 minutes. Sprinkle with the reserved Cheddar cheese. Bake for 5 minutes longer.

# Onion-Roasted Potatoes

2 pounds potatoes, coarsely chopped
1/2 cup olive oil or vegetable oil

1 envelope onion soup mix

Combine the potatoes, olive oil and soup mix in a sealable plastic bag. Shake the bag until the potatoes are evenly coated. Pour the potato mixture into a baking pan or roasting pan. Bake at 450 degrees, for 40 minutes or until the potatoes are tender and golden brown, stirring occasionally. Garnish with chopped fresh parsley.

# Glazed Acorn Squash with Walnuts

3 acorn squash
1/4 cup (1/2 stick) margarine
1/2 cup coarsely chopped walnuts

1/4 cup packed brown sugar
2 tablespoons maple syrup

Cut each squash into halves lengthwise; remove the seeds. Cut the squash into 1-inch-thick slices crosswise. Arrange the squash in a 9×13-inch baking dish. Bake, covered, at 350 degrees for 35 to 40 minutes or until almost tender. Melt the margarine in a saucepan over medium heat. Stir in the walnuts, brown sugar and maple syrup. Cook just until the brown sugar is dissolved. Spoon over the squash. Bake for 10 to 15 minutes longer or until squash is tender, basting occasionally.

# Southern Fried Squash

1 cup self-rising cornmeal
1 cup self-rising flour

2 squash, sliced
1/4 cup canola oil

Combine the cornmeal and flour in a sealable plastic bag and shake to mix. Add the squash and shake to coat the squash. Heat the canola oil in a skillet over medium heat. Arrange the squash in the skillet. Cook until brown on both sides, turning once.

Baked Squash Casserole

3 pounds yellow summer squash,
  chopped
1/2 cup chopped onion
1/2 cup cracker meal or bread crumbs
2 eggs

1/2 cup (1 stick) butter, melted
1 tablespoon sugar
1 teaspoon salt or to taste
1/2 teaspoon pepper or to taste
Cracker meal or bread crumbs

Combine the squash and enough water to cover in a saucepan. Bring to a boil over medium-high heat. Boil until the squash is tender; drain well. Mash the squash in a bowl. Add the onion, 1/2 cup cracker meal, eggs, half the butter, sugar, salt and pepper and mix well. Spoon into a baking dish. Sprinkle with the remaining butter and cracker meal. Bake at 375 degrees for 1 hour or until brown.

Sweet Potato Soufflé

4 cups mashed cooked sweet potatoes
1 cup sugar
1/2 cup (1 stick) margarine
2 eggs
1 teaspoon vanilla extract

1 cup packed brown sugar
1 cup chopped nuts
1/3 cup flour
1/3 cup butter

Combine the sweet potatoes, sugar, margarine, eggs and vanilla in a bowl and mix well. Spoon into a buttered baking dish. Combine the brown sugar, nuts, flour and butter and mix well. Sprinkle over the top of the sweet potato mixture. Bake at 350 degrees for 30 minutes.

calloped Tomato Casserole

3¹/2 cups chopped peeled tomatoes
1 cup chopped onion
¹/2 cup cheese-flavored cracker crumbs
1¹/2 teaspoons sugar

¹/2 teaspoon salt
1 cup sour cream
1¹/2 cups seasoned croutons
1 tablespoon butter, melted

Layer the tomatoes, onion, cracker crumbs, sugar and salt half at a time in a 1¹/2-quart baking dish. Bake at 325 degrees for 20 minutes. Spread the sour cream over the top. Sprinkle with the croutons and melted butter. Bake for 10 minutes longer.

omato Gravy

3 tablespoons bacon drippings
2 tablespoons flour
2 medium or 3 small fresh tomatoes,
   chopped

Salt and pepper to taste

Heat the bacon drippings in an 8- or 10-inch skillet over medium heat. Add the flour and mix well. Cook until light brown, stirring constantly. Add the tomatoes, salt and pepper and mix well. Cook until thickened, stirring constantly.

ried Green Tomatoes

1/2 cup cup flour
1/2 cup cornmeal
1 teaspoon salt
1 teaspoon pepper

1/2 teaspoon sugar to taste
3 green tomatoes, chilled, thickly sliced
2 eggs, beaten
1/4 cup vegetable oil

Combine the flour, cornmeal, salt, pepper and sugar in a shallow bowl. Coat the tomatoes with the flour mixture. Dip in the egg and coat with the flour mixture again. Heat the vegetable oil in a skillet over medium-high heat. Cook the tomatoes in the hot oil for 2 minutes per side or until brown. Remove to paper towels to drain.

urnip Greens

1 large bunch turnip greens
2 quarts water
1/4 pound salt pork or ham hock

1 teaspoon salt
Pinch of sugar
Butter (optional)

Rinse the turnip greens in cold salted water; drain. Rinse and drain the turnip greens. Remove and discard tough stems. Combine the water and salt pork in a 3-quart saucepan. Cook, covered, for 20 minutes. Add the turnip greens, 1 teaspoon salt and sugar. Cook for 1 to 1 1/2 hours or until most of the liquid has evaporated. Season with butter just before serving.

Breads

Basic Biscuits

2 cups self-rising flour, sifted
1/4 cup shortening

2/3 cup buttermilk

Place the flour in a medium bowl and cut in the shortening with a pastry cutter. Add the buttermilk gradually, stirring until the dough holds together. Roll 1/2 inch thick on a floured surface and cut with a biscuit cutter or pinch off small amounts of dough and roll into small balls. Press the balls into 1/2-inch-thick ovals. Place 2 inches apart on a greased baking pan. Bake at 450 degrees for 10 to 12 minutes or until golden brown.

Angel Biscuits

1 envelope dry yeast
2 tablespoons warm water
5 cups (or more) flour, sifted
1 teaspoon baking soda
1 tablespoon baking powder

1/4 cup sugar
1 teaspoon salt
1 cup shortening
1 1/2 to 2 cups buttermilk
Melted butter

Dissolve the yeast in the warm water in a small bowl. Sift 5 cups of the flour, the baking soda, baking powder, sugar and salt into a large bowl. Cut in the shortening until crumbly. Add 1 1/2 cups of the buttermilk and the yeast mixture gradually, mixing well after each addition. Stir in enough of the remaining buttermilk or add additional flour, as necessary, to make a soft dough that can be easily worked.

Knead gently on a floured surface until smooth and elastic and roll 1/2 inch thick. Cut with a biscuit cutter and brush with melted butter. Place on a lightly greased baking sheet, far apart for crisp-sided biscuits or close together for soft-sided biscuits. Bake at 400 degrees for 12 to 15 minutes or until golden brown. You may refrigerate the dough for several days before baking.

arlic Cheese Biscuits

2 cups baking mix
2/3 cup milk
3/4 cup shredded Cheddar cheese

1/4 cup (1/2 stick) margarine, melted
1/4 teaspoon garlic powder

Combine the baking mix, milk and cheese in a mixing bowl, stirring until a soft dough forms. Beat vigorously for 30 seconds. Drop by spoonfuls onto an ungreased baking sheet. Bake at 450 degrees for 8 to 10 minutes or until golden brown. Combine the margarine and garlic powder in a small bowl and mix well. Brush the warm biscuits with the margarine mixture. Serve warm.

our Cream Rolls or Biscuits

1 cup (2 sticks) butter, softened
2 cups self-rising flour

1 heaping cup sour cream

Combine the butter and flour in a large bowl and stir to mix. Add the sour cream and mix well. Drop by spoonfuls into greased miniature muffin cups or knead and roll out the dough on a floured surface and cut with small biscuit cutters. Bake at 400 degrees until golden brown. Serve with jellies for breakfast, as the bread course at a luncheon or stuffed with ham for a reception.

orn Bread

2 cups self-rising cornmeal
1 cup buttermilk
2 eggs

1/2 cup vegetable oil
1 tablespoon sugar

Combine the cornmeal, buttermilk, eggs, vegetable oil and sugar in a large bowl and mix well. Pour into a greased baking pan, cast-iron skillet or muffin cups. Bake at 400 degrees until golden brown. Cool on a wire rack.

ream-Style Corn Bread

1 (8-ounce) can cream-style corn
1 cup sour cream
1/2 cup vegetable oil

1 cup self-rising cornmeal
2 eggs

Grease a cast-iron skillet and heat in a 400-degree oven. Combine the corn, sour cream, vegetable oil, cornmeal and eggs in a large bowl and mix well. Pour into the hot skillet. Bake at 400 degrees for 20 minutes or until golden brown. Cool slightly on a wire rack. Cut into wedges and serve.

ush Puppies

1¹/2 cups self-rising cornmeal
¹/2 cup self-rising flour
1 egg, beaten

6 tablespoons chopped onion
2 cups buttermilk
Peanut oil for deep-frying

Whisk the cornmeal and flour together in a large bowl. Combine the egg, onion and 1¹/2 cups of the buttermilk in a bowl and mix well. Add to the dry ingredients and mix well, adding enough of the remaining buttermilk to make of the desired consistency. Drop by tablespoonfuls into hot deep peanut oil. Fry until the hush puppies float. Remove with a slotted spoon and drain on paper towels. Serve with fried fish.

pple Nut Bread

1¹/2 cups vegetable oil
2 cups sugar
3 eggs
2 teaspoons vanilla extract
3 cups flour

1 teaspoon baking soda
1 teaspoon salt
3 cups chopped peeled cored apples
1 cup chopped nuts

Combine the vegetable oil, sugar, eggs and vanilla in a large bowl and whisk to blend. Sift the flour, baking soda and salt together. Add to the egg mixture and mix well. Stir in the apples and nuts. Divide the batter evenly between 2 or 3 greased loaf pans or pour into a greased 9×13-inch baking pan. Bake at 350 degrees for 1 hour. Cool on a wire rack.

Apricot Banana Bread

1/3 cup butter or margarine, softened
2/3 cup sugar
2 eggs
1 cup mashed bananas
1/4 cup buttermilk
11/4 cups flour

1 teaspoon baking powder
1/2 teaspoon baking soda
1/2 teaspoon salt
1 cup 100% bran cereal
3/4 cup chopped dried apricots
1/2 cup chopped walnuts

Cream the butter and sugar in a mixing bowl until light and fluffy. Add the eggs and mix well. Combine the bananas and buttermilk in a bowl and mix well. Sift the flour, baking powder, baking soda and salt together. Add to the creamed mixture alternately with the banana mixture, mixing well after each addition. Stir in the cereal, apricots and walnuts. Spoon into a greased 5×9-inch loaf pan. Bake at 350 degrees for 55 to 60 minutes or until the loaf tests done. Cool in the pan for 10 minutes. Remove to a wire rack to cool completely.

Banana Nut Bread

1/2 cup (1 stick) margarine, softened
1 cup sugar
2 eggs
2 cups self-rising flour

1 teaspoon baking soda
3 bananas, mashed
1 cup chopped nuts

Cream the margarine and sugar in a mixing bowl until light and fluffy. Add the eggs and mix well. Sift the flour and baking soda together. Add to the creamed mixture and mix well. Stir in the bananas and nuts. Pour into a greased loaf pan. Bake at 350 degrees for 1 hour and 10 minutes. Cool in the pan for 10 minutes. Remove to a wire rack to cool completely.

ranberry Nut Bread

2 cups sifted flour
1 cup sugar
1 1/2 teaspoons baking powder
1/2 teaspoon baking soda
1 teaspoon salt
1/4 cup shortening

3/4 cup orange juice
1 tablespoon grated orange zest
1 egg, beaten
1/2 cup chopped nuts
1 cup cranberries, coarsely chopped

Sift the flour, sugar, baking powder, baking soda and salt into a large bowl. Cut in the shortening until the mixture resembles coarse cornmeal. Combine the orange juice, orange zest and egg in a small bowl and whisk to blend. Add to the flour mixture and mix just until moistened. Fold in the nuts and cranberries gently. Spoon into a greased 5×9-inch loaf pan and spread the batter slightly higher at the corners and sides than in the center. Bake at 350 degrees for 1 hour or until a wooden pick inserted in the center comes out clean. Remove from the pan and cool on a wire rack. Store overnight for easier slicing.

ate Nut Bread

2 cups dates, cut into large pieces
1/2 teaspoon salt
1 teaspoon baking soda
1 tablespoon butter or margarine
1 cup boiling water

1 egg
1 cup sugar
2 cups flour
1 cup chopped walnuts or pecans

Place the dates in a medium bowl and sprinkle with the salt and baking soda. Add the butter. Pour the boiling water over the mixture and set aside. Beat the egg with the sugar in a medium bowl. Add the flour alternately with the liquid from the dates, mixing well after each addition. Fold in the dates and walnuts. Spoon into a greased and floured 5×9-inch loaf pan. Bake at 350 degrees for 1 hour. Cool in the pan for 10 minutes. Remove from the pan and cool completely on a wire rack.

range Walnut Bread

2¹/2 cups flour
1¹/4 cups sugar
2 teaspoons baking powder
1/2 teaspoon baking soda
1/2 teaspoon salt
2 eggs, beaten

1/4 cup (1/2 stick) margarine, melted
1/2 cup orange juice
2 tablespoons grated orange zest
2 tablespoons water
1 cup English walnuts, chopped
1/4 cup flaked coconut (optional)

Combine the flour, sugar, baking powder, baking soda and salt in a large bowl and whisk to blend. Combine the eggs, margarine, orange juice, orange zest and water in a bowl and mix well. Add to the dry ingredients and stir quickly just until moistened. Stir in the walnuts and coconut. Pour into a greased and floured 5×9-inch loaf pan. Bake at 350 degrees for 1 hour or until bread tests done. Cool in the pan for 10 minutes. Remove to a wire rack to cool completely.

aisin Bread

2¹/4 cups boiling water
1 (15-ounce) package raisins
1 tablespoon shortening
2 cups sugar

2 eggs
4¹/2 cups flour
1 tablespoon baking soda
1¹/4 teaspoons salt

Pour the boiling water over the raisins in a medium bowl and let stand for 15 minutes. Combine the shortening, sugar and eggs in a mixing bowl and mix well. Sift the flour, baking soda and salt together. Add to the sugar mixture with the raisin mixture and mix well. Divide the batter evenly among 3 greased 1-pound coffee cans or 2 greased loaf pans. Bake at 300 degrees for 1¹/4 to 1¹/2 hours or until bread tests done. Cool in the cans for 10 minutes. Remove to a wire rack to cool completely.

pricot Muffins

1 cup boiling water
1 cup chopped dried apricots
1/2 cup (1 stick) butter or margarine,
  softened
1 cup sugar
1 cup sour cream

2 cups flour
1 teaspoon baking soda
1/2 teaspoon salt
1 tablespoon grated orange zest
1/2 cup chopped nuts

Pour the boiling water over the apricots in a bowl and let stand for 5 minutes. Cream the butter and sugar in a bowl until light and fluffy. Add the sour cream and mix well. Sift the flour, baking soda and salt together. Add to the creamed mixture and mix just until moistened. Drain the apricots, discarding the liquid. Fold in the apricots, orange zest and nuts. Divide the batter evenly among 12 greased or paper-lined muffin cups. Bake at 400 degrees for 18 to 20 minutes or until muffins test done. Cool in the pan for 10 minutes. Remove to a wire rack to cool completely.

anana Crumb Muffins

1 1/2 cups flour
1 teaspoon baking soda
1 teaspoon baking powder
1/2 teaspoon salt
3 large bananas, mashed
3/4 cup sugar

1 egg, lightly beaten
1/3 cup butter or margarine, melted
1/3 cup packed brown sugar
1 tablespoon flour
1/8 teaspoon cinnamon
1 tablespoon butter or margarine

Sift 1 1/2 cups flour, baking soda, baking powder and salt into a large bowl. Combine the bananas, sugar, egg and 1/3 cup butter in a bowl and mix well. Add to the dry ingredients and stir just until moistened. Divide the batter evenly among 12 greased or paper-lined muffin cups. Whisk the brown sugar, 1 tablespoon flour and cinnamon together in a small bowl. Cut in 1 tablespoon butter until crumbly. Sprinkle over the batter in the muffin cups. Bake at 375 degrees for 18 to 20 minutes or until muffins test done. Cool in the pan for 10 minutes. Remove to a wire rack to cool completely.

anana Nut Muffins

2 cups flour
1/4 cup sugar
1 tablespoon baking powder
1/2 teaspoon salt
1 cup milk

1 egg, beaten
1/3 cup vegetable oil
3/4 cup mashed banana
1/2 cup chopped walnuts or pecans

Sift the flour, sugar, baking powder and salt into a medium bowl and make a well in the center. Combine the milk, egg, vegetable oil and banana in a bowl and whisk to blend. Pour into the well in the flour mixture and stir just until moistened. Fold in the walnuts gently. Divide the batter evenly among 12 greased muffin cups. Bake at 400 degrees for 15 minutes or until the muffins are golden brown and a wooden pick inserted in the center of one of the muffins comes out clean. Cool on a wire rack. Substitute blueberries or raisins for the mashed banana if desired.

lueberry Muffins

1 3/4 cups flour
2 1/2 teaspoons baking powder
3/4 teaspoon salt
3/4 cup sugar

1/3 cup vegetable oil
1/2 cup milk
1 egg
1 cup fresh or frozen blueberries

Whisk the flour, baking powder, salt and sugar together in a large bowl. Combine the vegetable oil, milk and egg in a small bowl and beat until smooth. Add to the flour mixture and mix just until moistened. Fold in the blueberries gently. Fill paper-lined muffin cups with the batter. Bake at 400 degrees for 20 to 30 minutes or until brown and crispy on top. Cool on a wire rack.

Chocolate Chip Mini-Muffins

1/2 cup sugar
1/4 cup shortening
1 egg
1/2 cup milk
1/2 teaspoon vanilla extract
1 cup flour

1/2 teaspoon baking soda
1/2 teaspoon baking powder
1/4 teaspoon salt
2/3 cup miniature semisweet
    chocolate chips

Cream the sugar and shortening in a bowl until light and fluffy. Add the egg, milk and vanilla and mix well. Sift the flour, baking soda, baking powder and salt together. Add to the creamed mixture gradually, mixing well after each addition. Fold in the chocolate chips. Spoon 1 tablespoon of the batter into each of 36 greased or paper-lined miniature muffin cups. Bake at 375 degrees for 10 to 13 minutes or until muffins test done. Cool in the pan for 10 minutes. Remove to a wire rack to cool completely.

Onion Cheese Muffins

1/2 cup chopped onion
3 tablespoons butter or margarine
3 cups flour
1 tablespoon baking powder
1 teaspoon salt

1/4 teaspoon pepper
1 1/2 cups milk
2 cups shredded Cheddar cheese
3 tablespoons chopped green chiles

Sauté the onion in the butter in a skillet until onion is tender but not brown; set aside. Whisk the flour, baking powder, salt and pepper together in a large bowl. Add the milk, cheese, green chiles and onion mixture and stir just until moistened; do not overmix. Fill each of 18 greased muffin cups 1/2 full. Bake at 350 degrees for 30 to 35 minutes or until muffins are brown and a wooden pick inserted in the center of one of the muffins comes out clean. Cool in the pan 5 minutes. Serve warm with soup or salad.

Maple Cream Sweet Rolls

1/2 cup packed light brown sugar	4 ounces cream cheese, softened
1/2 cup chopped pecans	1 tablespoon margarine, softened
1/4 cup maple syrup	2 tablespoons confectioners' sugar
2 tablespoons margarine, melted	1 (10-count) can biscuits

Combine the brown sugar, pecans, maple syrup and 2 tablespoons margarine in a bowl and mix well. Spread over the bottom of an ungreased 8-inch square baking pan. Beat the cream cheese, 1 tablespoon margarine and confectioners' sugar in a mixing bowl until fluffy. Roll each biscuit into a 4-inch circle. Place 1 rounded teaspoon of the cream cheese mixture across the center of each circle to within 1/4 inch of the edge. Fold the dough over the filling, forming each into a log-shaped roll. Place the rolls, seam side down, in rows over the brown sugar mixture. Bake at 350 degrees for 25 minutes or until deep golden brown. Cool in the pan for 5 minutes. Invert onto a serving plate.

Hot Rolls

2 envelopes dry yeast	2/3 cup butter, softened
1/2 cup warm water	5 cups flour
1/2 cup warm milk	1 teaspoon salt
2 eggs	Melted butter
1/2 cup sugar	

Dissolve the yeast in the water and milk in a large bowl. Add the eggs, sugar and 2/3 cup butter and stir to combine. Whisk the flour and salt together in a bowl. Add to the yeast mixture gradually, mixing until the mixture forms a dough. Place the dough in a greased bowl and brush the top of the dough with melted butter. Let rise until doubled in bulk. Punch the dough down and knead briefly on a floured surface. Roll out and cut into 24 equal pieces. Place the rolls side by side in a baking pan and brush the tops with additional melted butter. Let rise until doubled in bulk. Bake at 350 degrees for 15 minutes. Cool on a wire rack. You may easily double this recipe.

innamon Twists

1 envelope dry yeast
3/4 cup warm water (110 to 115 degrees)
4 to 4 1/2 cups flour
1/4 cup sugar
1 1/2 teaspoons salt
1/2 cup warm milk (110 to 115 degrees)
1/4 cup (1/2 stick) butter or margarine,
  softened

1 egg
1/4 cup (1/2 stick) butter or margarine,
  melted
1/2 cup packed brown sugar
4 teaspoons cinnamon

Dissolve the yeast in 1/4 cup of the warm water in a large mixing bowl. Add 2 cups of the flour, sugar, salt, milk, 1/4 cup butter, egg and remaining water and beat at medium speed for 2 minutes. Stir in enough of the remaining flour to make a soft dough. Knead on a floured surface for 6 to 8 minutes or until smooth and elastic. Place in a greased bowl, turning to coat the surface. Let rise, covered, in a warm place for 1 hour or until doubled in bulk.

Punch the dough down and roll into a 12×16-inch rectangle on a lightly floured surface. Brush with 1/4 cup melted butter. Whisk the brown sugar and cinnamon together in a bowl. Sprinkle evenly over the dough and let stand for 6 minutes. Cut lengthwise into three 4×16-inch strips. Cut each strip into sixteen 1×4-inch pieces. Twist each piece and arrange on greased baking sheets. Let rise, covered, for 30 minutes or until doubled in bulk. Bake at 350 degrees for 15 minutes or until golden brown. Cool slightly and serve.

Sour Cream Coffee Cake

1 cup (2 sticks) margarine, softened
2 cups sugar
2 eggs
1/2 teaspoon vanilla extract
2 cups flour
1 teaspoon baking powder

1/4 teaspoon salt
1 cup sour cream
3/4 cup chopped pecans
3 tablespoons sugar
1 teaspoon cinnamon

Cream the margarine and 2 cups sugar in a mixing bowl until light and fluffy. Add the eggs and vanilla and beat to blend. Sift the flour, baking powder and salt together. Add to the creamed mixture alternately with the sour cream, beginning and ending with the flour mixture and mixing well after each addition. Pour half the batter into a greased bundt pan. Combine the pecans, 3 tablespoons sugar and cinnamon in a bowl and mix well. Sprinkle half the pecan mixture evenly over the batter in the pan. Top with the remaining batter and sprinkle with the remaining pecan mixture. Bake at 350 degrees for 50 to 60 minutes or until coffee cake tests done. Cool in the pan for 10 minutes. Invert onto a serving plate.

Mushroom Bread

1 (8-count) can crescent rolls
2 cups sliced fresh mushrooms
3 tablespoons butter or margarine, melted

1/4 cup grated Parmesan cheese
1/4 teaspoon Italian seasoning

Unroll the crescent roll dough. Place on a baking sheet and pinch the seams together. Toss the mushrooms in the butter to coat. Arrange evenly over the top of the dough. Sprinkle with the cheese and Italian seasoning. Bake at 375 degrees for 20 to 25 minutes or until golden brown. Cut into wedges or squares with a pizza cutter and serve warm.

Cakes

Banana Cake

2 small bananas, sliced
1 (2-layer) package yellow cake mix
1 (4-ounce) package banana cream
   instant pudding mix

4 eggs
1 cup water
1/4 cup vegetable oil
1/2 cup finely chopped nuts

Place the bananas in a large mixing bowl and beat until well mashed. Add the cake mix, pudding mix, eggs, water and vegetable oil and beat at low speed. Beat at medium speed for 2 minutes, scraping the side of the bowl 1 or 2 times. Fold in the nuts and pour into a greased and floured 10-inch tube pan or bundt pan.

Bake at 350 degrees for 1 hour or until cake tests done. Cool in the pan for 15 minutes. Invert onto a wire rack to cool completely. You may also bake this cake in a greased and floured 9×13-inch cake pan for 50 to 55 minutes.

Ooey-Gooey Butter Cake

1 (16-ounce) package pound cake mix
1/2 cup (1 stick) butter or margarine,
   melted
4 eggs

8 ounces cream cheese, softened
1 1/4 cups confectioners' sugar
1 cup chopped pecans
1 cup semisweet chocolate chips

Combine the cake mix, butter and 2 of the eggs in a mixing bowl and beat at medium speed until smooth. Pour into a lightly greased 9×13-inch cake pan. Combine the remaining eggs, cream cheese and 1 cup of the confectioners' sugar in a mixing bowl and beat at medium speed until smooth. Pour over the cake batter in the prepared pan. Sprinkle evenly with the pecans and chocolate chips.

Bake at 350 degrees for 30 to 40 minutes or until a wooden pick inserted in the center comes out clean. Cool in the pan on a wire rack. Sift the remaining confectioners' sugar evenly over the top.

hocolate Dream Cake

1 (2-layer) package fudge cake mix
  (without pudding)
1 envelope whipped topping mix
4 eggs

1 cup water
1 teaspoon vanilla extract
1 teaspoon butter flavoring
Sour Cream Chocolate Frosting

Combine the cake mix, whipped topping mix, eggs, water, vanilla and butter flavoring in a mixing bowl and beat at medium speed for 4 minutes. Pour into 2 greased and floured 9-inch round cake pans. Bake at 325 degrees for 35 minutes or until a wooden pick inserted in the center comes out clean. Cool in the pans for 10 minutes. Remove to a wire rack to cool completely. Spread the Sour Cream Chocolate Frosting between the layers and over the top and side of the cooled cake.

Sour Cream Chocolate Frosting

2 cups semisweet chocolate chips
1/2 cup sour cream

1 1/2 cups sifted confectioners' sugar
4 to 5 tablespoons milk

Place the chocolate chips in the top of a double boiler over boiling water. Reduce the heat to low and cook until the chocolate melts, stirring frequently; cool. Combine the chocolate and sour cream in a mixing bowl and mix well. Add the confectioners' sugar alternately with the milk, beating at medium speed until smooth and of the desired spreading consistency.

Milk Chocolate Bar Cake

1 (2-layer) package Swiss chocolate cake
   mix
8 ounces cream cheese, softened
1 cup confectioners' sugar

$^{1}\!/_{2}$ cup sugar
10 (1- to 2-ounce) milk chocolate candy
   bars with almonds
12 ounces whipped topping

Prepare and bake the cake mix using the package directions for three 8-inch round cake pans. Beat the cream cheese, confectioners' sugar and sugar in a mixing bowl at medium speed until creamy. Chop 8 of the candy bars finely. Place the whipped topping in a bowl. Fold the cream cheese mixture and chopped candy bars into the whipped topping.

Spread the mixture between the layers and over the top and side of the cooled cake. Chop the remaining candy bars. Sprinkle half the chopped candy over the top of the cake and press the remaining chopped candy along the bottom edge of the cake.

Black Forest Cake

1 (2-layer) package Swiss chocolate
   cake mix
24 ounces cream cheese, softened

1 (1-pound) package confectioners' sugar
1 (21-ounce) can cherry pie filling

Prepare and bake the cake mix using the package directions for two 9-inch round cake pans. Slice the cooled layers in half horizontally. Combine the cream cheese and confectioners' sugar in a mixing bowl and beat until smooth and creamy. Spread the mixture evenly over 3 of the cake layers, stacking the layers. Place the remaining cake layer on top and spread with the pie filling. Refrigerate until ready to serve.

erman Chocolate Cake

1 (2-layer) package German chocolate
    cake mix
3 eggs
1 1/2 cups water
1/3 cup vegetable oil

1 (14-ounce) can sweetened condensed
    milk
1 (12-ounce) jar caramel topping
8 ounces whipped topping
3 toffee candy bars, crushed

Combine the cake mix, eggs, water and vegetable oil in a mixing bowl and beat until smooth. Pour into a greased 9×13-inch cake pan. Bake at 350 degrees for 35 to 40 minutes or until a wooden pick inserted in the center comes out clean. Prick holes in the hot cake with a wooden spoon handle. Pour the sweetened condensed milk and caramel topping over the cake. Cool for 1 hour. Spread with the whipped topping and sprinkle evenly with the crushed candy bars. Refrigerate until serving time.

urtle Cake

1 (2-layer) package German chocolate
    cake mix (with pudding)
1 (14-ounce) package caramel candies
1/2 cup (1 stick) butter or margarine

1/3 cup milk
3/4 cup milk chocolate chips
1 cup chopped pecans

Prepare the cake mix using the package directions. Spoon half the batter into a greased and floured 9×13-inch cake pan. Bake at 350 degrees for 10 minutes; set aside. Combine the caramel candies, butter and milk in a medium saucepan. Cook over low heat until the caramel candies melt, stirring constantly.

Spread the mixture over the cake and sprinkle evenly with the chocolate chips and pecans. Spread the remaining cake batter evenly over the top. Bake at 350 degrees for 20 to 25 minutes. Cool slightly. Cut into squares to serve. May substitute dry-roasted peanuts for the pecans.

Earthquake Cake

1 (2-layer) package German chocolate
  cake mix
1 1/2 cups flaked coconut
1 1/2 cups chopped pecans

1/2 cup (1 stick) margarine, softened
8 ounces cream cheese, softened
4 cups confectioners' sugar

Prepare the cake mix using the package directions. Sprinkle the coconut and pecans over the bottom of a greased 9×13-inch cake pan. Pour the prepared cake batter over the top. Combine the margarine, cream cheese and confectioners' sugar in a mixing bowl and beat until smooth and creamy. Drop by spoonfuls over the batter in the pan. Bake at 350 degrees for 45 minutes or until cake tests done. Cool on a wire rack.

Coconut Cake

1 (2-layer) package yellow cake mix
1 (14-ounce) can sweetened
  condensed milk

1 (8- to 9-ounce) can cream of coconut
16 ounces whipped topping
1 (3- to 4-ounce) can flaked coconut

Prepare and bake the cake mix using the package directions for a 9×13-inch cake pan. Cool on a wire rack for 15 minutes. Poke several holes in the cake using a wooden spoon handle. Combine the sweetened condensed milk and cream of coconut in a bowl and mix well. Pour over the cake and let stand overnight. Spread evenly with the whipped topping and sprinkle with the coconut. Store leftovers in the refrigerator.

Coconut Rave Cake

2 cups flaked coconut
Butter
1 (2-layer) package yellow cake mix
1 (4-ounce) package vanilla instant
  pudding mix

1 1/3 cups water
4 eggs
1/4 cup vegetable oil
1 cup chopped nuts
Coconut Frosting

Toast the coconut in a small amount of butter in a medium skillet over medium heat until golden brown, stirring constantly. Combine the cake mix, pudding mix, water, eggs and vegetable oil in a large mixing bowl and beat for 4 minutes. Stir in the toasted coconut and nuts. Divide the batter evenly among 3 greased and floured 9-inch round cake pans.

Bake at 350 degrees for 35 minutes. Cool in the pans for 15 minutes. Remove to a wire rack to cool completely. Spread the Coconut Frosting between the layers and over the top and side of the cake.

Coconut Frosting

6 tablespoons margarine, softened
12 ounces cream cheese, softened
5 cups confectioners' sugar
1 teaspoon vanilla extract

3 cups flaked coconut, toasted
Milk
Chopped nuts

Combine the margarine, cream cheese, confectioners' sugar and vanilla in a mixing bowl and beat until smooth and creamy. Stir in the coconut and enough milk to make of the desired spreading consistency. Stir in the nuts.

Coconut Sheet Cake

1 (2-layer) package yellow cake mix
1 cup sweetened condensed milk
1 cup sugar

8 ounces whipped topping
1 (7-ounce) package flaked coconut

Prepare and bake the cake mix using the package directions for a 9×13-inch cake pan. Combine the sweetened condensed milk and sugar in a saucepan and bring to a boil, stirring constantly. Pour over the hot cake and let stand to cool completely. Spread with the whipped topping and sprinkle with the coconut. Store leftovers in the refrigerator.

Lemon Gelatin Cake

1 (2-layer) package yellow cake mix
1 (3-ounce) package lemon gelatin
3/4 cup vegetable oil
3/4 cup apricot nectar
4 egg yolks

2 teaspoons lemon extract
4 egg whites, stiffly beaten
2 cups confectioners' sugar
Juice of 2 lemons
Grated zest of 1 lemon

Combine the cake mix, gelatin, vegetable oil, apricot nectar, egg yolks and lemon extract in a bowl and beat until smooth and creamy. Fold in the egg whites gently. Pour into a greased and floured tube pan. Bake at 325 degrees for 1 hour. Cool in the pan for 10 minutes. Invert onto a serving plate. Combine the confectioners' sugar, lemon juice and lemon zest in a bowl and mix well. Pour evenly over the hot cake and let stand until cool.

range Crunch Cake

1 cup graham cracker crumbs
1/2 cup packed brown sugar
1/2 cup chopped pecans
1/2 cup (1 stick) margarine, melted
1 (2-layer) package yellow cake mix
1/2 cup water
1/2 cup orange juice

3 eggs
1/2 cup vegetable oil
1 (16-ounce) can vanilla frosting
1 cup whipped topping
1 (11-ounce) can mandarin oranges,
  drained

For the crunch layer, combine the graham cracker crumbs, brown sugar, pecans and margarine in a bowl and mix until crumbly. Pour into 2 greased and floured 8- or 9-inch round cake pans.

For the cake, combine the cake mix, water, orange juice, eggs and vegetable oil in a mixing bowl and beat at low speed until moistened. Beat at high speed for 2 minutes. Pour the batter over the crunch layer in each pan. Bake at 350 degrees for 30 to 35 minutes or until the cake tests done. Cool in the pans for 10 minutes. Remove to a wire rack to cool completely.

For the frosting, beat the vanilla frosting in a mixing bowl until fluffy. Add the whipped topping and continue beating until light and fluffy. Spread the frosting between the cake layers, crunch side up, and over the top and side of the cooled cake. Arrange the oranges decoratively over the top and refrigerate until serving time.

Orange Cake

1 (2-layer) package orange cake mix
1/3 cup sugar
2 tablespoons flour
1 cup sour cream
2/3 cup vegetable oil
1/2 teaspoon orange extract

4 eggs
1 (11-ounce) can mandarin oranges,
    drained
1 cup confectioners' sugar
2 tablespoons orange juice

Sift the cake mix, sugar and flour together. Combine the sour cream, vegetable oil, orange extract and eggs in a large bowl and whisk to blend. Add the sifted dry ingredients and beat until smooth. Fold in the mandarin oranges. Pour into a greased and floured bundt pan. Bake at 350 degrees for 45 to 50 minutes or until cake tests done. Cool in the pan for 10 minutes. Invert onto a serving plate. Combine the confectioners' sugar and orange juice in a small bowl and mix well. Drizzle over the warm cake.

Orange Pineapple Cake

1 (2-layer) package butter golden cake mix
1/2 cup (1 stick) butter, softened
3/4 cup cold milk
3 eggs
2 cups whipping cream, whipped

1 (20-ounce) can crushed pineapple
1 (4-ounce) package vanilla instant
    pudding mix
1 (11-ounce) can mandarin oranges,
    drained

Combine the cake mix, butter, milk and eggs in a mixing bowl. Beat at low speed until moistened, scraping the side of the bowl and the beaters 1 or 2 times. Beat at medium speed for 3 minutes; do not overmix. Divide the batter evenly among 3 lightly greased and floured 9-inch round cake pans.

Bake at 325 degrees for 25 minutes or until cake tests done. Cool in the pans for 10 minutes. Remove to a wire rack to cool completely. Combine the whipped cream, pineapple and pudding mix in a mixing bowl and beat at medium speed just until well mixed. Spread between the layers and over the top of the cake. Arrange the orange slices decoratively over the top and refrigerate until serving time.

 Mountain Dew Cake

1 (2-layer) package lemon or yellow cake
  mix
1 (6-ounce) package vanilla instant
  pudding mix
10 ounces Mountain Dew or Sprite
  (1¼ cups)

3/4 cup vegetable oil
4 eggs
Pineapple Frosting

Combine the cake mix, pudding mix, Mountain Dew, vegetable oil and eggs in a mixing bowl and beat for 4 minutes. Divide the batter evenly among 3 greased and floured 9-inch round cake pans.

Bake at 325 degrees for 30 to 35 minutes or until cake tests done. Cool in the pans for 10 minutes. Remove to a wire rack to cool completely. Spread the Pineapple Frosting between the layers and over the top and side of the cake.

Pineapple Frosting

1 (20-ounce) can crushed pineapple
1 cup sugar
2 eggs, beaten

1/2 cup (1 stick) margarine
1 tablespoon self-rising flour
1 cup flaked coconut

Combine the pineapple, sugar, eggs, margarine and flour in a saucepan and cook until the margarine has melted and the mixture has thickened, stirring frequently. Remove from the heat and stir in the coconut. Set aside to cool.

ineapple Coconut Cake

1 (4-ounce) package French vanilla
   instant pudding mix
1 (2-layer) package white cake mix
1 (20-ounce) can crushed pineapple,
   drained

1 cup flaked coconut
1 cup chopped pecans or macadamia
   nuts, toasted
8 ounces whipped topping

Prepare the pudding mix using the package directions. Chill for 1 hour. Prepare and bake the cake mix using the package directions for a 9×13-inch cake pan. Cool in the pan on a wire rack. Spread the pudding over the cooled cake. Spoon the pineapple over the top and sprinkle with the coconut and 1/2 of the pecans. Spread with the whipped topping and sprinkle with the remaining pecans. Chill, covered, for 8 hours or overnight.

ineapple Upside-Down Cake

1/4 cup (1/2 stick) butter or margarine
1 cup packed light brown sugar
8 slices drained canned pineapple

1 (2-layer) package white cake mix
8 maraschino cherries (optional)

Melt the butter in a 10-inch cast-iron skillet. Remove from the heat and sprinkle the brown sugar evenly over the melted butter. Arrange the pineapple slices over the brown sugar. Prepare the cake mix using the package directions. Pour the batter over the pineapple. Bake at 350 degrees for 45 minutes or until the cake pulls away from the side of the skillet. Cool in the skillet for 5 minutes. Invert onto a serving plate. Place 1 cherry in the center of each pineapple slice and serve.

oppy Seed Pound Cake

1 (2-layer) package yellow cake mix
1 (4-ounce) package vanilla instant
   pudding mix
1/2 cup sugar
1/4 cup poppy seeds

1/2 cup sour cream
3 eggs, beaten
1/2 cup vegetable oil
1/2 cup sherry
1 teaspoon vanilla extract

Whisk the cake mix, pudding mix, sugar and poppy seeds together in a large bowl. Combine the sour cream, eggs, vegetable oil, sherry and vanilla in a medium bowl and beat until well mixed. Pour into the dry ingredients and mix well. Pour the batter into a greased and floured tube or bundt pan. Bake at 350 degrees for 50 minutes or until the cake is brown. Cool in the pan for 15 minutes. Invert onto a serving plate. Glaze as desired.

um Cake

1 (2-layer) package yellow cake mix
1 (4-ounce) package vanilla instant
   pudding mix
4 eggs
1/2 cup rum
1/2 cup water

1/2 cup vegetable oil
1 cup chopped pecans
1 cup sugar
1/2 cup (1 stick) butter, softened
1/4 cup rum
1/4 cup water

Combine the cake mix, pudding mix, eggs, 1/2 cup rum, 1/2 cup water and vegetable oil in a mixing bowl and beat until smooth. Sprinkle the pecans into a greased and floured bundt pan. Pour the batter over the pecans. Bake at 325 degrees for 45 to 50 minutes or until cake tests done. Combine the sugar, butter, 1/4 cup rum and 1/4 cup water in a saucepan and bring to a boil. Boil for 2 to 3 minutes, stirring constantly. Pour over the warm cake in the pan and let stand for 30 minutes. Invert onto a serving plate.

*S*trawberry Coconut Pecan Cake

1 (2-layer) package white cake mix
1 (3-ounce) package strawberry gelatin
1 cup vegetable oil
1/2 cup milk
4 eggs

1 cup frozen strawberries, thawed
1 cup flaked coconut
1 cup chopped pecans
Strawberry Pecan Frosting

Whisk the cake mix and gelatin together in a large bowl. Add the vegetable oil and milk and mix well. Add the eggs 1 at a time, beating after each addition. Fold in the undrained strawberries, coconut and pecans. Divide the batter evenly among 3 greased 8-inch round cake pans.

Bake at 350 degrees for 40 to 45 minutes or until cake tests done. Cool in the pans for 10 minutes. Remove to a wire rack to cool completely. Spread the Strawberry Pecan Frosting between the layers and over the top and side of the cake.

Strawberry Pecan Frosting

1/2 cup (1 stick) margarine, softened
1 (1-pound) package confectioners' sugar
1/2 cup flaked coconut

1/2 cup frozen strawberries, thawed, drained
1/2 cup chopped pecans

Cream the margarine and confectioners' sugar in a mixing bowl. Add the coconut, strawberries and pecans and mix well.

 Strawberry Cake

1 (2-layer) package white cake mix
1 (3-ounce) package strawberry gelatin
4 eggs
1/2 cup water
1/2 cup vegetable oil

1 (10-ounce) package frozen strawberries,
    thawed
1 (1-pound) package confectioners' sugar
1/4 cup (1/2 stick) butter, melted

Whisk the cake mix and gelatin together in a bowl. Add the eggs 1 at a time, mixing well after each addition. Add the water and vegetable oil and mix well. Fold in half the strawberries. Pour into 2 greased and floured 9-inch round cake pans.

Bake at 350 degrees for 30 minutes or until cake tests done. Cool in the pans for 10 minutes. Remove to a wire rack. Blend the confectioners' sugar with the butter in a bowl until smooth. Drain the remaining strawberries and fold into the frosting mixture. Spread the frosting between the layers and over the top and side of the warm cake.

 Basic Layer Cake

2 cups sifted cake flour
1 cup sugar
1 tablespoon baking powder
1/4 teaspoon salt
1/2 cup (1 stick) butter, softened

2/3 cup milk
2 teaspoons vanilla extract
4 egg yolks
Caramel Pecan Frosting (page 136)

Sift the flour, sugar, baking powder and salt into a large mixing bowl. Add the butter, milk and vanilla and beat at low speed until well mixed. Beat at medium speed for 2 minutes. Add the egg yolks 1 at a time, beating well after each addition. Divide the batter evenly among 3 greased and floured 9-inch round cake pans. Bake at 325 degrees for 20 to 25 minutes or until cake tests done. Cool in the pans for 10 minutes. Remove to a wire rack to cool completely. Frost with Caramel Pecan Frosting or as desired.

Buttermilk Layer Cake

1 cup shortening
2 cups sugar
3 eggs
2 1/2 cups flour
1/2 teaspoon salt

1/2 teaspoon baking soda
1 1/2 cups buttermilk
2 teaspoons vanilla extract
Caramel Frosting (page 135) or
    Caramel Pecan Frosting (page 136)

Beat the shortening in a mixing bowl at medium speed until creamy. Add the sugar gradually, beating constantly. Add the eggs 1 at a time, beating well after each addition. Sift the flour, salt and baking soda together. Add to the shortening mixture alternately with the buttermilk and vanilla, beginning and ending with the flour mixture and beating at low speed after each addition. Beat at medium-high speed for 2 minutes.

Divide the batter evenly among 3 greased and floured 8-inch round cake pans. Bake at 350 degrees for 22 minutes or until a wooden pick inserted in the center comes out clean. Cool in the pans for 10 minutes. Remove to a wire rack to cool completely. Frost with Caramel Frosting or Caramel Pecan Frosting.

Quick-Mix Two-Egg Cake

2 1/4 cups sifted self-rising flour
1 1/2 cups sugar
1/2 cup shortening

1 cup milk
1 teaspoon vanilla extract
2 eggs

Sift the flour and sugar into a bowl. Add the shortening and half the milk and mix well. Beat with an electric mixer for 2 minutes. Add the remaining milk, vanilla and eggs and beat for 2 minutes. Pour into 2 greased 9-inch round cake pans. Bake at 350 degrees for 30 minutes or until cake tests done. Cool in the pans for 10 minutes. Remove to a wire rack to cool completely. Frost as desired.

ane Cake

1 cup (2 sticks) butter, softened
1 3/4 cups sugar
1 cup milk
1 teaspoon vanilla extract

3 cups flour
1 tablespoon baking powder
8 egg whites, stiffly beaten
Coconut Pecan Frosting

Cream the butter and sugar in a mixing bowl until light and fluffy. Add the milk and vanilla and mix well.

Sift the flour and baking powder together. Add to the creamed mixture and mix well. Fold in the egg whites gently.

Pour into 3 greased and floured 9-inch round cake pans. Bake at 325 degrees for 20 to 25 minutes or until cake tests done. Cool in the pans for 10 minutes. Remove to a wire rack to cool completely.

Spread the Coconut Pecan Frosting between the layers and over the top and side of the cake.

Coconut Pecan Frosting

8 egg yolks, beaten
1 cup sugar
1 tablespoon flour
1 cup (2 sticks) butter, softened

1/3 cup milk
1 cup chopped pecans
2 cups flaked coconut

Combine the egg yolks, sugar, flour, butter and milk in the top of a double boiler and mix well. Cook over simmering water for 5 minutes or until thickened, stirring constantly. Remove from the heat and stir in the pecans and coconut. Let stand until cool.

Southern Apple Cake

1 1/2 cups vegetable oil
2 cups sugar
3 eggs
2 teaspoons vanilla extract
3 cups flour
1 teaspoon salt

1 teaspoon baking soda
1 teaspoon cinnamon
1 cup coarsely chopped pecans
3 cups chopped peeled cored apples
1 cup packed brown sugar
6 tablespoons margarine, softened

Combine the vegetable oil, sugar, eggs and vanilla in a large bowl and mix well. Sift the flour, salt, baking soda and cinnamon together. Add to the egg mixture and blend until smooth. Stir in the pecans and apples. Pour into a greased and floured tube pan. Bake at 350 degrees for 1 hour. Combine the brown sugar and margarine in a small saucepan and bring to a boil, stirring constantly. Boil for 3 minutes, stirring constantly. Pour over the hot cake in the pan. Let stand for 2 hours. Invert onto a serving plate.

Apple Cake with Caramel Topping

2 cups sugar
1 1/2 cups vegetable oil
3 eggs
2 tablespoons vanilla extract
3 cups flour
Cinnamon to taste

3 apples, peeled, cored, chopped
1 to 1 1/2 cups chopped nuts
1/4 cup evaporated milk
1/2 cup (1 stick) butter
1 cup packed brown sugar
1 tablespoon vanilla extract

Combine the sugar and vegetable oil in a large bowl and mix well. Add the eggs 1 at a time, mixing well after each addition. Stir in 2 tablespoons vanilla. Sift the flour and cinnamon together. Add to the egg mixture and mix well. Stir in the apples and nuts. Pour into a greased 9×13-inch cake pan. Bake at 325 degrees for 1 hour or until deeply golden brown. Place the pan on a wire rack. Combine the milk, butter and brown sugar in a saucepan and bring to a boil, stirring until the butter is melted and the brown sugar is dissolved. Remove from the heat and stir in 1 tablespoon vanilla. Let stand for 3 minutes. Pour over the warm cake in the pan.

arvelous Banana Cake

1 cup (2 sticks) butter or margarine,
   softened
3 cups sugar
2 cups mashed bananas
4 eggs, beaten
3³/4 cups flour

2 teaspoons baking soda
1 cup buttermilk
1 teaspoon vanilla extract
2 tablespoons orange juice
1 cup chopped pecans
Banana Nut Frosting

Cream the butter in a mixing bowl. Add the sugar gradually, beating at medium speed until light and fluffy. Add the bananas and beat until smooth. Stir in the eggs. Sift the flour and baking soda together. Add to the banana mixture alternately with the buttermilk, beginning and ending with the flour mixture and mixing well after each addition. Stir in the vanilla, orange juice and pecans. Divide the batter evenly among 3 greased and floured 9-inch round cake pans.

Bake at 350 degrees for 35 to 40 minutes or until a wooden pick inserted in the center comes out clean. Cool in the pans for 10 minutes. Remove to a wire rack to cool completely. Spread the Banana Nut Frosting between the layers and over the top and side of the cooled cake.

Banana Nut Frosting

1/2 cup mashed banana
1 teaspoon lemon juice
1/3 cup butter or margarine, softened
1 (1-pound) package plus 3 cups
   confectioners' sugar, sifted

3 to 4 tablespoons milk
1 cup flaked coconut, toasted
2/3 cup finely chopped pecans

Combine the banana and lemon juice in a bowl and mix well; set aside. Beat the butter in a mixing bowl at medium speed until creamy. Add the confectioners' sugar and milk and mix well. Add the banana mixture and beat until fluffy. Stir in the coconut and pecans.

Hummingbird Cake

3 cups flour
1 teaspoon baking soda
1 teaspoon salt
1 teaspoon cinnamon
2 cups sugar
3 eggs, beaten

1¹/2 cups vegetable oil
1¹/2 teaspoons vanilla extract
1 (8-ounce) can crushed pineapple
2 cups chopped bananas
2¹/2 cups chopped pecans
Cream Cheese Frosting

Whisk the flour, baking soda, salt, cinnamon and sugar together in a large bowl. Add the eggs and vegetable oil and stir just until the dry ingredients are moistened; do not beat. Stir in the vanilla, undrained pineapple, bananas and 2 cups of the pecans. Divide the batter evenly among 3 greased and floured 9-inch round cake pans.

Bake at 350 degrees for 25 to 30 minutes or until a wooden pick inserted in the center comes out clean. Cool in the pans for 10 minutes. Remove to a wire rack to cool completely. Spread the Cream Cheese Frosting between the layers and over the top and side of the cake. Sprinkle the remaining pecans over the top of the frosted cake.

Cream Cheese Frosting

8 ounces cream cheese, softened
¹/2 cup (1 stick) margarine, softened

1 teaspoon vanilla extract
1 (1-pound) package confectioners' sugar

Cream the cream cheese and margarine in a mixing bowl until fluffy. Add the vanilla and confectioners' sugar and beat until smooth and creamy.

Caramel Cake

1 cup (2 sticks) butter, softened
2 cups sugar
4 eggs
3 cups sifted flour
1 teaspoon salt

1 tablespoon baking powder
1 cup milk
$^1/_2$ teaspoon vanilla extract
$^1/_4$ teaspoon almond extract
Burnt Caramel Frosting

Cream the butter and sugar in a mixing bowl until very fluffy. Add the eggs 1 at a time, beating well after each addition. Sift the flour, salt and baking powder together 3 times. Add to the creamed mixture alternately with the milk, beating well after each addition. Stir in the vanilla and almond extract. Divide the batter evenly among 3 greased and floured 9-inch round cake pans.

Bake at 325 degrees for 25 minutes or until a cake tester inserted in the center comes out clean. Cool in the pans for 5 to 10 minutes. Remove to a wire rack to cool completely. Spread the Burnt Caramel Frosting between the layers and over the top and side of the cake.

Burnt Caramel Frosting

$^1/_4$ cup sugar
$^1/_4$ teaspoon baking soda
$^1/_4$ cup hot water

3 cups sugar
1 cup evaporated milk
$^1/_2$ cup (1 stick) margarine, softened

Brown $^1/_4$ cup sugar in a saucepan over high heat, stirring constantly. Mix the baking soda and hot water in a small bowl and quickly pour over the browned sugar, stirring constantly. Remove from the heat and add 3 cups sugar, evaporated milk and margarine. Cook over medium heat until thickened and bubbly, stirring constantly.

aramel Walnut Cake

1 cup sugar
1 (1-pound) package brown sugar
1¹/2 cups shortening
5 eggs
2¹/2 cups flour
1 teaspoon baking powder

1/2 teaspoon salt
1 cup milk
1 tablespoon vanilla extract
1¹/2 cups chopped English walnuts
1/2 cup flour
Buttermilk Frosting

Cream the sugar, brown sugar and shortening in a large mixing bowl until light and fluffy. Add the eggs 1 at a time, mixing well after each addition. Sift 2¹/2 cups flour, baking powder and salt together 3 times. Add to the creamed mixture alternately with the milk and vanilla, mixing well after each addition. Toss the walnuts with 1/2 cup flour in a small bowl. Stir the mixture into the batter.

Pour into a greased and floured tube pan. Bake at 325 degrees for 1¹/2 to 1³/4 hours or until cake tests done. Cool in the pan for 15 minutes. Invert onto a serving plate to cool completely. Spread with the Buttermilk Frosting.

Buttermilk Frosting

1 cup sugar
1/2 teaspoon baking soda
1/2 cup buttermilk

1 tablespoon dark or light corn syrup
1¹/4 teaspoons vanilla extract
1/2 cup (1 stick) butter, softened

Combine the sugar, baking soda, buttermilk, corn syrup, vanilla and butter in a medium saucepan and bring to a boil, stirring constantly. Cook for 5 minutes or until of the desired spreading consistency, stirring constantly.

Fabulous Carrot Cake

2 cups flour
2 cups sugar
2 teaspoons cinnamon
1 teaspoon baking powder
1/2 teaspoon baking soda
1/2 teaspoon salt

1 1/2 cups vegetable oil
4 eggs, beaten
1 teaspoon vanilla extract
2 cups grated carrots
Cream Cheese Pecan Icing

Sift the flour, sugar, cinnamon, baking powder, baking soda and salt into a large bowl. Combine the vegetable oil, eggs and vanilla in a medium bowl and whisk to blend. Add to the sifted dry ingredients and mix well. Stir in the carrots. Divide the batter evenly among 3 greased and floured 9-inch round cake pans.

Bake at 350 degrees for 20 to 25 minutes or until cake tests done. Cool in the pans for 10 minutes. Remove to a wire rack to cool completely. Spread the Cream Cheese Pecan Icing between the layers and over the top and side of the cake. You may bake the cake in a greased 9×13-inch cake pan if desired.

Cream Cheese Pecan Icing

1/2 cup (1 stick) margarine, softened
8 ounces cream cheese, softened
1 (1-pound) package confectioners' sugar

2 teaspoons vanilla extract
1 cup chopped pecans

Cream the margarine and cream cheese in a bowl until light and fluffy. Add the confectioners' sugar and vanilla and mix well. Stir in the pecans.

German Sweet Chocolate Cake

4 ounces German's sweet chocolate
1/2 cup boiling water
1 cup (2 sticks) butter or margarine,
　softened
2 cups sugar
4 egg yolks
1 teaspoon vanilla extract

2 1/2 cups flour
1 teaspoon baking soda
1/2 teaspoon salt
1 cup buttermilk
4 egg whites, stiffly beaten
Coconut Pecan Frosting

Melt the chocolate in the boiling water in a bowl; cool. Cream the butter and sugar in a mixing bowl until light and fluffy. Add the egg yolks 1 at a time, beating well after each addition. Blend in the chocolate mixture and vanilla. Sift the flour, baking soda and salt together. Add to the creamed mixture alternately with the buttermilk, beating after each addition until smooth. Fold in the egg whites gently.

Divide the batter evenly among 3 greased and floured 9-inch round cake pans. Bake at 350 degrees for 30 to 35 minutes or until cake tests done. Cool in the pans for 10 minutes. Remove to a wire rack to cool completely. Spread the Coconut Pecan Frosting between the layers and over the top and side of the cake.

Coconut Pecan Frosting

1 cup evaporated milk
1 cup sugar
3 egg yolks, lightly beaten
1/2 cup (1 stick) butter or margarine

1 teaspoon vanilla extract
1 1/3 cups flaked coconut
1 cup chopped pecans

Combine the evaporated milk, sugar, egg yolks, butter and vanilla in a medium saucepan. Cook over medium heat for 12 minutes or until the butter has melted and the mixture has thickened, stirring constantly. Stir in the coconut and pecans and set aside to cool until the mixture is thick and of the desired spreading consistency.

hocolate Sheet Cake

2 cups flour
2 cups sugar
1/2 teaspoon salt
3 tablespoons baking cocoa
1/3 cup vegetable oil
1/2 cup (1 stick) margarine, softened

1 cup water
2 eggs
1/2 cup buttermilk
1 teaspoon baking soda
1 teaspoon vanilla extract
Cocoa Frosting

Sift the flour, sugar and salt into a mixing bowl. Combine the baking cocoa, vegetable oil, margarine and water in a medium saucepan and bring to a boil, stirring constantly. Pour over the flour mixture and stir until well mixed. Add the eggs, buttermilk, baking soda and vanilla and mix well. Pour into a greased 10×15-inch sheet cake pan. Bake at 350 degrees for 25 minutes. Spread the Cocoa Frosting evenly over the hot cake.

Cocoa Frosting

1/2 cup (1 stick) butter
1 teaspoon vanilla extract
6 tablespoons milk

2 tablespoons baking cocoa
1 (1-pound) package confectioners' sugar
1 cup chopped nuts

Melt the butter in a saucepan over low heat. Add the vanilla, milk and baking cocoa and mix well. Remove from the heat and add the confectioners' sugar and nuts and stir until well mixed.

Marshmallow Fudge Squares

1 cup shortening
2 cups sugar
4 eggs
1 tablespoon vanilla extract
1 1/2 cups flour

1/3 cup baking cocoa
1/3 teaspoon salt
1 (6-ounce) package miniature
  marshmallows
Buttery Cocoa Frosting

Cream the shortening and sugar together in a mixing bowl until light and fluffy. Add the eggs and vanilla and beat for 30 seconds. Sift the flour, baking cocoa and salt together. Add to the creamed mixture and beat until well combined. Pour into a greased and floured 9×13-inch glass baking dish.

Bake at 300 degrees for 35 minutes. Remove from the oven and scatter the miniature marshmallows evenly over the top. Bake for 5 minutes longer. Cool on a wire rack in the pan for 15 minutes. Spread evenly with the Buttery Cocoa Frosting and let stand for 2 hours before cutting into squares to serve.

Buttery Cocoa Frosting

1 cup (2 sticks) butter, softened
1/2 cup baking cocoa
1 (1-pound) package confectioners' sugar

1 teaspoon vanilla extract
1/2 cup evaporated milk

Combine the butter, baking cocoa, confectioners' sugar and vanilla in a mixing bowl and beat until smooth and creamy. Add the evaporated milk gradually, beating constantly until of the desired spreading consistency.

Mississippi Mud Cake

1 cup (2 sticks) butter or margarine,
    softened
2 cups sugar
1/2 cup baking cocoa
4 eggs
11/2 cups cake flour

Dash of salt
1 teaspoon vanilla extract
11/2 cups chopped pecans
1 (6-ounce) package miniature
    marshmallows
Mississippi Mud Icing

Cream the butter, sugar and baking cocoa in a mixing bowl until light and fluffy. Add the eggs 1 at a time, beating well after each addition. Add the cake flour, salt and vanilla and mix well. Stir in the pecans. Pour into a greased and floured 9×13-inch cake pan. Bake at 325 degrees for 40 minutes. Remove from the oven and scatter the marshmallows evenly over the cake. Bake for 5 minutes longer or until the marshmallows melt. Cool on a wire rack for 15 minutes. Spread the Mississippi Mud Icing evenly over the warm cake. Cool for several hours before cutting.

Mississippi Mud Icing

1/4 cup (1/2 stick) butter, softened
1 (1-pound) package confectioners' sugar

1/4 cup baking cocoa
1 teaspoon vanilla extract

Cream the butter in a mixing bowl until light and fluffy. Add the confectioners' sugar and baking cocoa and beat until well mixed. Stir in the vanilla.

Italian Cream Cake

1/2 cup (1 stick) margarine, softened
1/2 cup shortening
2 cups sugar
5 egg yolks
2 cups flour
1 teaspoon baking soda

1 cup buttermilk
1 teaspoon vanilla extract
1/2 (12-ounce) package frozen coconut
1 cup chopped pecans
5 egg whites, stiffly beaten
Cream Cheese Frosting (page 118)

Cream the margarine and shortening in a mixing bowl until smooth. Beat in the sugar until smooth. Add the egg yolks and mix well. Sift the flour and baking soda together. Add to the creamed mixture alternately with the buttermilk. Stir in the vanilla, coconut and pecans. Fold in the egg whites gently. Pour into 3 greased and floured 9-inch round cake pans. Bake at 350 degrees for 25 minutes or until cake tests done. Cool in the pans for 10 minutes. Remove to a wire rack to cool completely. Frost with Cream Cheese Frosting.

Coconut Cake

1 recipe Basic Layer Cake (page 113) or
    Buttermilk Layer Cake (page 114)
1 1/2 (12-ounce) packages frozen coconut,
    thawed, or 4 1/2 cups flaked coconut,
    finely chopped
1 cup sour cream

1 cup sugar
1 1/2 teaspoons vanilla extract
2 cups whipping cream
1/4 cup sifted confectioners' sugar
1/4 cup sugar

Prepare and bake the cake; cool completely. Combine 2/3 of the coconut, the sour cream, 1 cup sugar and 1 teaspoon of the vanilla in a bowl and mix well; set aside. Beat the whipping cream, confectioners' sugar and remaining vanilla together in a mixing bowl until soft peaks form. Combine the remaining coconut and 1/4 cup sugar in a bowl and mix well; set aside.

Place 1 cake layer on a serving plate. Spread with half the sour cream mixture. Top with 1 cake layer and spread with the remaining sour cream mixture. Top with the remaining cake layer. Spread the whipped cream mixture over the top and side of the entire cake. Sprinkle the top and side of the cake with the coconut-sugar mixture, patting gently to ensure the mixture adheres to the cake. Chill before serving. Refrigerate leftovers.

$\mathcal{L}$uscious Coconut Cake

1 cup (2 sticks) unsalted butter, softened
2 cups sugar
3 cups flour
1 cup buttermilk
4 eggs
1/2 cup buttermilk
1 teaspoon baking soda
1 teaspoon vanilla extract

1 teaspoon coconut extract
Pinch of salt
1 cup sugar
1 cup milk
1 teaspoon coconut extract
White Mountain Frosting
2 (12-ounce) packages frozen coconut, thawed

Cream the butter and 2 cups sugar in a mixing bowl until light and fluffy. Add the flour and 1 cup buttermilk and mix well. Add the eggs 1 at a time, beating well after each addition. Combine 1/2 cup buttermilk with the baking soda and add to the creamed mixture, stirring to blend. Stir in the vanilla, 1 teaspoon coconut extract and salt. Divide the mixture evenly among 3 greased and floured 9-inch round cake pans.

Bake at 325 degrees for 30 minutes or until cake tests done. Cool slightly in the pans on a wire rack. Combine 1 cup sugar, the milk and 1 teaspoon coconut extract in a small saucepan and simmer over medium heat for 5 minutes, stirring constantly. Remove from the heat. Poke holes in the cake layers with the tines of a fork. Spoon the glaze evenly over each warm layer. Remove the layers from the pans. Spread White Mountain Frosting over each layer and top each with a portion of the coconut. Stack the layers and frost the top and side of the cake with White Mountain Frosting. Sprinkle the top and side of the cake with the remaining coconut.

White Mountain Frosting

1 cup sugar
1/4 cup water
1/2 cup light corn syrup

4 egg whites
1 teaspoon vanilla extract or coconut extract

Combine the sugar, water and corn syrup in a saucepan and mix well. Cover the saucepan and bring the mixture to a rolling boil. Remove the cover and cook for 2 minutes or until the mixture spins a 6- to 8-inch thread, stirring constantly; do not overcook. Beat the egg whites in a bowl until stiff peaks form. Pour the hot syrup mixture into the egg whites slowly, beating constantly until the frosting holds peaks. Stir in the vanilla.

apanese Fruit Cake

1 cup (2 sticks) butter, softened
2 cups sugar
4 eggs, beaten
2 cups (or more) flour
2 teaspoons baking powder
1 cup buttermilk

1 teaspoon allspice
1 teaspoon cinnamon
1 teaspoon ground cloves
1 cup raisins
1 cup chopped pecans (optional)
Apple Filling

Cream the butter and sugar in a mixing bowl until light and fluffy. Add the eggs and mix well. Sift the flour and baking powder together. Add to the creamed mixture alternately with the buttermilk, mixing well after each addition. Stir in additional flour, if necessary, to make a stiff batter. Pour 1/3 of the cake batter into a separate bowl and add the allspice, cinnamon, cloves, raisins and pecans, stirring until well mixed. Pour into a greased and floured 9-inch round cake pan. Divide the remaining batter between 2 greased and floured 9-inch round cake pans.

Bake the 3 layers at 350 degrees for 40 minutes or until cake tests done. Cool in the pans for 10 minutes. Remove to a wire rack to cool completely. Spread the Apple Filling over each cooled cake layer and stack the layers, placing the spiced layer in the middle.

Apple Filling

2 cups sugar
3 to 4 tablespoons flour
2 oranges, peeled, seeded, grated
1 cup boiling water

2 apples, peeled, cored, grated
1 cup chopped pecans
1 cup flaked coconut (optional)
1 cup raisins (optional)

Combine the sugar, flour, oranges and boiling water in a saucepan and stir until well mixed. Stir in the apples, pecans, coconut and raisins. Cook until thickened, stirring frequently.

Southern Peanut Cake

2 1/2 cups flour
1 2/3 cups sugar
1 1/4 teaspoons baking powder
1 teaspoon baking soda
1 teaspoon salt
2/3 cup shortening

1/2 cup buttermilk
1 cup mashed banana
1/3 cup buttermilk
2 eggs
1 cup ground roasted peanuts
Peanut Frosting

Sift the flour, sugar, baking powder, baking soda and salt into a large bowl. Add the shortening, 1/2 cup buttermilk and banana and beat vigorously for 2 minutes. Add 1/3 cup buttermilk and eggs and beat for 2 minutes longer. Stir in the peanuts. Divide the batter evenly among 3 greased and floured 9-inch round cake pans.

Bake at 375 degrees for 25 minutes. Cool in the pan for 10 minutes. Remove to a wire rack to cool completely. Spread the Peanut Frosting between the layers and over the top and side of the cake.

Peanut Frosting

1/2 cup (1 stick) butter
3 cups confectioners' sugar
1 cup ground roasted peanuts

1 to 2 teaspoons evaporated milk or
   cream

Soften the butter in the top of a double boiler over simmering water. Add the confectioners' sugar and peanuts and stir until well mixed. Stir in enough of the evaporated milk to make of the desired spreading consistency.

ed Velvet Cake

2 cups vegetable oil
1¹/2 cups sugar
2 eggs
2¹/2 cups flour
1 tablespoon baking cocoa
1 teaspoon baking soda

1 teaspoon salt
1 cup buttermilk
1 teaspoon vinegar
1 small bottle red food coloring
1 teaspoon vanilla extract
Cream Cheese Pecan Icing (page 121)

Cream the vegetable oil and sugar in a mixing bowl. Add the eggs and mix well. Sift the flour, baking cocoa, baking soda and salt together. Add to the creamed mixture and mix well. Add the buttermilk, vinegar, red food coloring and vanilla and mix until well blended. Divide the batter evenly among 3 greased and floured 9-inch round cake pans.

Bake at 325 degrees for 25 to 30 minutes or until cake tests done. Cool in the pans for 10 minutes. Remove to a wire rack to cool completely. Spread the Cream Cheese Pecan Icing between the layers and over the top and side of the cake.

ruit Cocktail Cake

2 cups self-rising flour
2 cups sugar
2 eggs
1 (15-ounce) can fruit cocktail
¹/4 cup (¹/2 stick) butter

1 cup sugar
1 cup milk
¹/2 cup chopped nuts
1 teaspoon vanilla extract

Combine the flour, 2 cups sugar, eggs and fruit cocktail in a large bowl and mix well. Pour into a greased and floured 9×13-inch cake pan. Bake at 325 degrees for 45 minutes or until cake tests done. Combine the butter, 1 cup sugar and the milk in a saucepan and bring to a boil, stirring constantly. Reduce the heat and cook for 10 minutes or until the butter is melted and the mixture is thickened. Remove from the heat and stir in the nuts and vanilla. Pour over the hot cake in the pan. Serve warm.

weet Potato Cake

1¹/2 cups vegetable oil
2 cups sugar
4 egg yolks
¹/4 cup hot water
2¹/2 cups cake flour
1 tablespoon baking powder
¹/4 teaspoon salt
1 teaspoon cinnamon

1 teaspoon nutmeg
1¹/2 cups grated peeled uncooked sweet
   potatoes
1 cup chopped pecans
1 teaspoon vanilla extract
4 egg whites, stiffly beaten
Coconut Filling

Combine the vegetable oil and sugar in a large mixing bowl and beat until smooth. Add the egg yolks and mix well. Stir in the hot water. Sift the flour, baking powder, salt, cinnamon and nutmeg together. Add to the egg mixture and mix well. Stir in the sweet potatoes, pecans and vanilla. Fold in the egg whites gently. Divide the batter evenly among 3 greased 8-inch round cake pans. Bake at 350 degrees for 25 to 30 minutes or until cake tests done. Remove from pans and cool on a wire rack. Spread the Coconut Filling between the layers and over the top of the cake.

Coconut Filling

1 (12-ounce) can evaporated milk
1 cup sugar
¹/2 cup (1 stick) butter or margarine,
   softened

3 tablespoons flour
1 teaspoon vanilla extract
1¹/3 cups flaked coconut

Combine the evaporated milk, sugar, butter, flour and vanilla in a saucepan. Cook over medium heat for 12 minutes or until thickened, stirring constantly. Remove from the heat and stir in the coconut. Beat until thickened and cooled.

Chocolate Pound Cake

1 cup (2 sticks) butter, softened
1/2 cup shortening
3 cups sugar
5 eggs
3 cups flour

1/2 cup baking cocoa
1/4 teaspoon baking powder
1 1/4 cups milk
1 teaspoon vanilla extract
Cocoa Icing

Cream the butter, shortening and sugar in a mixing bowl until light and fluffy. Add the eggs 1 at a time, beating well after each addition. Sift the flour, baking cocoa and baking powder together. Add to the creamed mixture alternately with a mixture of the milk and vanilla, mixing well after each addition. Pour into a greased and floured tube pan. Bake at 300 degrees for 1 hour and 25 minutes or until cake tests done. Cool in the pan for 10 minutes. Remove to a wire rack to cool completely. Spread with the Cocoa Icing.

Cocoa Icing

2 cups sugar
1/4 cup baking cocoa
1/4 teaspoon salt

2/3 cup milk
1/2 cup shortening
1 tablespoon vanilla extract

Combine the sugar, baking cocoa, salt, milk and shortening in a saucepan and bring to a boil, stirring constantly. Boil for 2 minutes, stirring constantly. Remove from the heat and stir in the vanilla. Beat until creamy.

even-Up Pound Cake

1¹/2 cups (3 sticks) margarine, softened
3 cups sugar
5 eggs
1 cup Seven-Up or Sprite
2 teaspoons vanilla extract
2 teaspoons lemon extract

3 cups flour
1/4 cup (1/2 stick) margarine, melted
1/2 (1-pound) package confectioners' sugar
2 tablespoons milk

Cream the softened margarine and sugar in a mixing bowl until light and fluffy. Add the eggs 1 at a time, beating well after each addition. Stir in the Seven-Up, half the vanilla and half the lemon extract. Add the flour and beat until smooth. Pour into a greased and floured tube pan. Bake at 325 degrees for 1¹/4 hours or until cake tests done.

Combine the melted margarine, confectioners' sugar, milk, remaining vanilla and remaining lemon extract in a bowl and beat until smooth. Pour over the hot cake in the pan. Cool on a wire rack. Invert onto a serving plate.

range Pound Cake

1 cup (2 sticks) butter, softened
1/2 cup shortening
3 cups sugar
6 eggs
3 cups flour

1/2 teaspoon baking powder
1/4 teaspoon salt
1 cup milk
2 teaspoons orange extract
1 teaspoon vanilla extract

Cream the butter, shortening and sugar in a mixing bowl until light and fluffy. Add the eggs 1 at a time, beating well after each addition. Beat for 3 minutes or longer. Sift the flour, baking powder and salt together. Add to the creamed mixture alternately with the milk, beating well after each addition. Stir in the orange extract and vanilla. Pour into a greased and floured tube pan. Place in a cold oven and set the oven temperature to 300 degrees. Bake for 1¹/2 hours or longer or until a toothpick inserted near the center of the cake comes out clean. Cool in the pan for 15 minutes. Invert onto a serving plate. You may substitute any flavor of choice for the orange extract.

ream Cheese Pound Cake

1¹/2 cups (3 sticks) butter, softened
8 ounces cream cheese, softened
3 cups sugar
6 jumbo eggs
3 cups flour

¹/2 teaspoon baking powder
2 teaspoons vanilla extract
¹/2 teaspoon coconut extract
¹/2 teaspoon almond extract

Cream the butter, cream cheese and sugar in a mixing bowl until light and fluffy. Add the eggs 1 at a time, beating well after each addition. Sift the flour and baking powder together. Add to the creamed mixture with the vanilla, coconut extract and almond extract. Mix until well blended. Pour into a greased and floured tube pan. Bake at 300 degrees for 2 hours. Cool in the pan for 10 minutes. Invert onto a serving plate.

Sour Cream Pound Cake

3 cups sugar
3 cups flour
1 cup shortening
1 cup sour cream
Pinch of salt
¹/4 teaspoon baking soda
6 eggs
1 teaspoon vanilla extract

1 teaspoon lemon extract
¹/4 cup (¹/2 stick) margarine, softened
¹/2 (1-pound) package confectioners'
   sugar
2 tablespoons milk
1 teaspoon vanilla extract
1 teaspoon lemon extract

Combine the sugar, flour, shortening, sour cream, salt, baking soda, eggs, 1 teaspoon vanilla and 1 teaspoon lemon extract in a large mixing bowl and beat for 4 minutes. Pour into a greased tube pan. Bake at 300 degrees for 1¹/2 hours or until cake tests done. Cool in the pan for 10 minutes. Invert onto a serving plate. Combine the margarine, confectioners' sugar, milk, 1 teaspoon vanilla and 1 teaspoon lemon extract in a bowl and beat until smooth. Drizzle the glaze over the hot cake.

Whipping Cream Pound Cake

1 cup (2 sticks) unsalted butter, whipped
3 cups sugar
6 eggs
3 cups flour

1 cup whipping cream
1 1/2 teaspoons vanilla or lemon extract,
  or 3/4 teaspoon of each

Cream the butter and sugar in a mixing bowl until light and fluffy. Add the eggs 1 at a time, beating well after each addition. Beat for 3 minutes. Add the flour alternately with a mixture of the whipping cream and vanilla, mixing well after each addition. Pour into a greased and floured tube pan. Place in a cold oven and set the oven temperature to 300 degrees. Bake for 2 hours or until cake tests done. Cool in the pan for 15 minutes. Invert onto a serving plate.

Caramel Frosting

3 3/4 cups sugar
1 1/2 cups heavy cream

1/4 cup (1/2 stick) butter
1/4 teaspoon baking soda

Combine 3 cups of the sugar, heavy cream, butter and baking soda in a heavy saucepan and bring to a boil, stirring constantly. Remove from the heat and keep warm. Sprinkle the remaining sugar in the bottom of a heavy saucepan. Cook over medium heat until the sugar melts and becomes a light golden brown syrup, stirring constantly. Pour into the cream mixture gradually, stirring until smooth. Cook over medium heat for 10 to 12 minutes or to 240 degrees on a candy thermometer, soft-ball stage, stirring frequently. Remove from the heat and beat at high speed with an electric mixer for 8 to 10 minutes or until the mixture is of the desired spreading consistency.

 Caramel Pecan Frosting

1 (12-ounce) jar caramel ice cream
    topping
1¹/2 cups (3 sticks) butter, softened

3 cups sifted confectioners' sugar
1 tablespoon vanilla extract
2 cups finely chopped pecans

Beat the caramel topping with the butter in a mixing bowl until smooth. Add the confectioners' sugar, vanilla and pecans gradually, beating until the frosting is creamy and of the desired spreading consistency. Use to frost Basic Layer Cake (page 113) or Buttermilk Layer Cake (page 114).

 Cooked Chocolate Frosting

2 cups sugar
¹/4 cup baking cocoa
¹/2 cup (1 stick) butter, softened

¹/2 cup milk
1 teaspoon vanilla extract

Combine the sugar, baking cocoa, butter and milk in a saucepan and bring to a boil, stirring constantly. Boil for 2 minutes, stirring constantly. Remove from the heat and stir in the vanilla; cool. Beat until of the desired spreading consistency.

Candy
&
Cookies

uttermilk Fudge

2 cups sugar
1 cup buttermilk
1/2 cup (1 stick) butter or margarine
1 teaspoon baking soda

2 tablespoons light corn syrup
1 teaspoon vanilla extract
3/4 cup chopped pecans

Combine the sugar, buttermilk, butter, baking soda and corn syrup in a buttered Dutch oven. Cook over medium heat to 234 degrees on a candy thermometer, soft-ball stage, stirring constantly. Remove from the heat and cool to 180 degrees. Stir in the vanilla. Beat at high speed until the mixture thickens and loses its luster. Stir in the pecans. Pour into a buttered 8-inch square baking pan; cool.

utterscotch Peanut Fudge

1 (11-ounce) package butterscotch chips
1 (14-ounce) can sweetened
  condensed milk
1 1/2 cups miniature marshmallows

2/3 cup chunky peanut butter
1 teaspoon vanilla extract
1/8 teaspoon salt
1 cup chopped dry-roasted peanuts

Combine the butterscotch chips, sweetened condensed milk and marshmallows in a small heavy saucepan. Cook over medium heat for 5 to 6 minutes, stirring constantly until smooth. Stir in the peanut butter, vanilla and salt. Stir in the peanuts. Pour into a buttered 9-inch square pan. Chill until firm. Cut into squares and serve. Store leftovers in the refrigerator.

ive Pounds of Chocolate Fudge

4 cups semisweet chocolate chips
1 cup (2 sticks) butter or margarine,
  softened
1 (7-ounce) jar marshmallow creme

4¹/2 cups sugar
1 (12-ounce) can evaporated milk
2 tablespoons vanilla extract
1¹/2 cups chopped pecans

Combine the chocolate chips, butter and marshmallow creme in a large bowl and mix well. Combine the sugar and evaporated milk in a buttered Dutch oven and mix well. Cook over medium heat to 234 degrees on a candy thermometer, soft-ball stage, stirring constantly. Pour over the chocolate mixture.

Beat at high speed with an electric mixer until the mixture thickens and loses its luster. Stir in the vanilla and pecans. Spread evenly in a buttered 10×15-inch baking pan. Chill until firm. Store in an airtight container at room temperature.

hocolate Nut Fudge

2¹/4 cups sugar
¹/4 cup (¹/2 stick) butter or margarine
1 cup marshmallow creme (about
  5 ounces)

³/4 cup evaporated milk
1 cup semisweet chocolate chips
1 cup chopped nuts

Combine the sugar, butter, marshmallow creme and evaporated milk in a heavy 2-quart saucepan. Bring to a full boil, stirring constantly. Boil over medium heat for 5 minutes, stirring constantly. Remove from the heat. Add the chocolate chips, stirring until melted. Stir in the nuts. Pour into a buttered 8- or 9-inch pan. Garnish with nut halves. Cool until set. Cut into very small pieces.

Rocky Road Fudge

1/2 cup (1 stick) margarine
2/3 cup baking cocoa
1/2 cup light corn syrup
1 tablespoon water

1 teaspoon vanilla extract
1 (1-pound) package confectioners' sugar
1 cup miniature marshmallows
1/2 cup chopped nuts

Melt the margarine in a 2-quart saucepan over low heat. Stir in the baking cocoa, corn syrup, water and vanilla. Remove from the heat and stir in the confectioners' sugar gradually, mixing until well blended and smooth. Stir in the marshmallows and nuts. Pour into a greased 8-inch square pan. Chill, covered, until firm. Cut into squares.

White Chocolate Fudge

6 ounces cream cheese, softened
1 (1-pound) package confectioners'
   sugar, sifted
1 1/2 teaspoons vanilla extract

1 (12-ounce) bar white baking chocolate,
   melted
1 cup chopped pecans

Beat the cream cheese at medium speed in a bowl until fluffy. Add the confectioners' sugar gradually, beating well after each addition. Add the vanilla and chocolate and stir until blended. Stir in the pecans. Spread in a buttered 8-inch square pan. Chill until firm.

Almond Peanut Clusters

2 pounds almond bark
2 cups chocolate chips

1 pound peanuts

Melt the almond bark in the top of a double boiler set over simmering water, stirring frequently. Add the chocolate chips and stir until melted and smooth. Remove from the heat and stir in the peanuts. Drop by teaspoonfuls onto waxed paper. Let stand until firm.

hocolate Mint Patties

1 (1-pound) package confectioners' sugar
1/4 cup baking cocoa
1/3 cup margarine, softened

1/3 cup light corn syrup
1 teaspoon peppermint extract

Sift the confectioners' sugar and baking cocoa together. Combine the margarine, corn syrup and peppermint extract in a large mixing bowl and beat at medium speed until well blended. Beat in 1 to 2 cups of the baking cocoa mixture until smooth. Stir in the remaining baking cocoa mixture with a wooden spoon. Knead the mixture until well blended and smooth. Shape into balls by teaspoonfuls. Flatten into patties. Store in a covered container in the refrigerator.

eanut Butter Logs

1 cup chunky peanut butter
1 cup confectioners' sugar
2 cups crisp rice cereal
1/2 cup chopped walnuts

2 tablespoons butter, softened
1 cup chocolate chips
2 tablespoons paraffin

Mix the first 5 ingredients in a bowl. Chill. Roll the mixture into 1-inch logs. Melt the chocolate and paraffin in a double boiler over boiling water until smooth, stirring constantly. Dip each log into the chocolate mixture and place on waxed paper. Let stand until firm.

eanut Clusters

16 ounces vanilla candy coating squares,
    coarsely chopped

2 2/3 cups milk chocolate chips
1 pound salted Spanish peanuts

Melt candy coating and chocolate chips in a heavy saucepan over low heat, stirring constantly. Remove from the heat and stir in peanuts. Drop by tablespoonfuls onto waxed paper-lined baking sheets. Chill for 30 minutes or until firm.

Pecan Clusters

1 (7-ounce) jar marshmallow creme
24 ounces milk chocolate kisses
5 cups sugar

1 (12-ounce) can evaporated milk
1/2 cup (1 stick) butter or margarine
6 cups pecan halves

Place the marshmallow creme and the chocolate kisses in a large bowl. Combine the sugar, evaporated milk and butter in a large heavy saucepan. Bring to a boil, stirring constantly. Boil for 8 minutes, stirring constantly. Pour over the marshmallow creme mixture and stir until the chocolate is melted. Stir in the pecan halves. Drop by rounded teaspoonfuls onto waxed paper-lined baking sheets. Chill for 2 hours or until firm. Store in the refrigerator.

Chocolate Pecan Candy

6 ounces unsweetened chocolate
1/4 block (or more) paraffin
1/2 cup (1 stick) margarine, melted

1 (1-pound) package confectioners' sugar
Pecan halves

Melt the chocolate with the paraffin in a small saucepan over low heat, stirring constantly. Remove from the heat and keep warm. Combine the margarine and confectioners' sugar in a bowl and stir until the mixture forms a dough. Place 2 pecan halves together and wrap with a small amount of dough, completely encasing the pecans. Repeat until all the dough is used.

Drop the pecan balls carefully, 1 at a time, into the chocolate mixture to coat. Remove with a slotted spoon and immediately press a pecan half into the top of each ball. Place the finished candies on a serving plate and refrigerate until serving time. Store leftovers in the refrigerator.

Texas Millionaires

1 (14-ounce) package caramel candies
2 tablespoons butter or margarine
2 tablespoons water

3 cups pecan halves
1 cup semisweet chocolate chips
16 ounces vanilla candy coating

Combine the caramel candies, butter and water in a heavy saucepan. Cook over low heat until melted and smooth, stirring constantly. Stir in the pecan halves. Remove from the heat and let stand for 5 minutes. Drop by tablespoonfuls onto lightly greased waxed paper. Chill for 1 hour or freeze for 20 minutes until firm.

Melt the chocolate chips and candy coating in a heavy saucepan over low heat, stirring until smooth. Dip the chilled candies, 1 at a time, into the chocolate mixture. Remove with a slotted spoon and place on lightly greased waxed paper. Let stand until firm.

Toasted Pecan Brittle

1¹/₂ cups pecan halves
1 cup sugar
¹/₂ cup light corn syrup
¹/₈ teaspoon salt

1 teaspoon vanilla extract
1 teaspoon butter
1 teaspoon baking soda

Place the pecans in a single layer on a baking sheet. Bake at 350 degrees for 8 minutes or until pecans are toasted, stirring occasionally. Combine the sugar, corn syrup, salt, vanilla and butter in a large heavy saucepan. Cook over medium heat until the mixture begins to darken, stirring gently and constantly. Add the toasted pecans and cook until golden brown, stirring constantly.

Remove from the heat and add the baking soda, stirring vigorously. Allow the foam to subside. Pour onto a 10×15-inch baking sheet with sides. Cool until set. Break into pieces. Store in an airtight container in a cool, dry place.

avorite Peanut Brittle

3 cups sugar
1 cup light corn syrup
1/2 cup water
3 cups raw peanuts

1 tablespoon butter
1 teaspoon salt
2 teaspoons baking soda

Combine the sugar, corn syrup and water in a heavy saucepan and mix well. Bring to a boil, stirring constantly. Cook to 250 degrees on a candy thermometer, spun-thread stage, stirring constantly. Add the peanuts and cook to 280 degrees, soft-crack stage, stirring constantly. Remove from the heat and stir in the butter, salt and baking soda until light and foamy. Pour onto a buttered board or baking sheet. Cool until firm. Break into pieces.

icrowave Peanut Brittle

2 cups sugar
1 cup light corn syrup
1 cup water
2 cups raw peanuts

1/2 teaspoon salt
1 tablespoon butter
1 teaspoon vanilla extract
1/2 teaspoon baking soda

Combine the sugar, corn syrup and water in a large microwave-safe bowl. Microwave on High for 5 to 6 minutes. Stir in the peanuts. Microwave on High for 3 to 5 minutes or until the corn syrup and peanuts are browned, stirring every 2 minutes. Stir in the salt. Add the butter, vanilla and baking soda and stir until light and foamy. Pour onto a large buttered baking sheet. Cool until firm. Break into pieces.

oconut Joys

¹/2 cup (1 stick) butter or margarine,
  melted
2 cups sifted confectioners' sugar

3 cups flaked coconut
¹/3 cup semisweet chocolate chips

Combine the butter, confectioners' sugar and coconut in a large bowl and mix well. Shape the mixture into 3/4-inch balls. Place on a baking sheet and chill for 30 minutes or until firm. Place the chocolate chips in a heavy-duty sealable plastic bag and seal the bag. Submerge the bag in hot water until the chocolate is melted. Snip a tiny hole in one corner of the bag. Drizzle the chocolate over the chilled coconut balls. Store in the refrigerator.

For microwave preparation, substitute 2 cups semisweet chocolate chips for the 1/3 cup chocolate chips in this recipe. Microwave the chocolate in a 2-cup glass measuring cup on High for 1 1/2 minutes or until melted. Dip the coconut balls into the chocolate and remove to waxed paper with a slotted spoon. Let stand until firm.

ate Nut Balls

3/4 cup (1¹/2 sticks) margarine
1 (1-pound) package dates, chopped
1 cup flaked coconut
1 cup chopped nuts

1 cup packed brown sugar
1 cup sugar
4 cups crisp rice cereal
Confectioners' sugar

Combine the margarine, dates, coconut, nuts, brown sugar and sugar in a large heavy saucepan. Cook over low heat until the margarine is melted and the sugars are dissolved, stirring constantly. Cool. Stir in the cereal. Shape the mixture into balls and roll in confectioners' sugar.

Divinity Honey Drops

2¹/2 cups sugar
¹/4 teaspoon salt
²/3 cup water
¹/4 cup honey

2 egg whites
1 teaspoon vanilla extract
1 or 2 drops food coloring (optional)

Combine the sugar, salt, water and honey in a heavy 2-quart saucepan. Bring the mixture to a boil over medium heat, stirring constantly. Reduce the heat and cook to 265 degrees on a candy thermometer, hard-ball stage; do not stir. Beat the egg whites in a mixing bowl until stiff peaks form. Add the hot syrup gradually, beating constantly. Beat until the mixture loses its luster and holds its shape when dropped from a spoon. Stir in the vanilla and desired food coloring. Drop by teaspoonfuls onto a lightly buttered baking sheet, swirling each piece to make a peak. Let stand until cool.

Holly Confections

¹/2 cup (1 stick) margarine
30 large marshmallows
2 teaspoons (about) green food coloring

3 cups cornflakes
Red hot cinnamon candies

Melt the margarine with the marshmallows in a large saucepan over low heat, stirring occasionally. Blend in the food coloring. Add the cornflakes and toss gently to coat. Drop by rounded tablespoonfuls onto waxed paper. Arrange the red hot cinnamon candies on the confections to resemble holly berries. Let stand until cool and firm.

aystacks

1 (11-ounce) package butterscotch chips
1 (5-ounce) can chow mein noodles

1/2 cup blanched peanuts

Melt the butterscotch chips in a saucepan over medium heat, stirring constantly. Remove from the heat and add the chow mein noodles and peanuts, stirring to coat. Drop by spoonfuls onto waxed paper. Let stand until set.

hite Christmas Candy

1 pound white bark candy
1 pound salted nuts

2 cups crisp rice cereal

Melt the white bark candy in the top of a double boiler over simmering water, stirring frequently. Add the nuts and cereal and mix well. Spoon onto a waxed paper-lined baking sheet and refrigerate until firm. Break into pieces. Store in an airtight container.

pricot Bars

1 cup (2 sticks) butter, softened
2 cups packed flour
3/4 cup sugar
1/2 cup chopped pecans

11/2 cups flaked coconut
11/2 cups apricot preserves
1 heaping tablespoon flour

Cream the butter, 2 cups flour and sugar in a mixing bowl. Stir in the pecans and coconut. Press 3/4 of the dough over the bottom of a 10×15-inch baking pan sprayed with nonstick cooking spray. Bake at 350 degrees for 12 minutes. Cool slightly. Spread evenly with the preserves. Add 1 heaping tablespoon flour to the remaining dough and stir until crumbly. Sprinkle over the preserves. Bake for 20 to 25 minutes longer or until browned. Cool in the pan on a wire rack. Cut into bars.

utterscotch Cheese Squares

1 (11-ounce) package butterscotch chips
1/3 cup margarine
2 cups graham cracker crumbs
1 cup chopped nuts
8 ounces cream cheese, softened

1 (14-ounce) can sweetened condensed milk
1 teaspoon vanilla extract
1 egg, beaten

Melt the butterscotch chips with the margarine in a medium saucepan over low heat, stirring frequently. Add the graham cracker crumbs and nuts and stir until crumbly. Press half the mixture over the bottom of a 9×13-inch baking pan. Combine the cream cheese, sweetened condensed milk, vanilla and egg in a bowl and beat until smooth and creamy. Spread evenly in the prepared pan. Top with the remaining graham mixture. Bake at 350 degrees for 25 minutes. Cool in the pan on a wire rack. Cut into squares.

hess Bars

1 (2-layer) package yellow cake mix
1 egg
1/2 cup (1 stick) butter or margarine, melted

8 ounces cream cheese, softened
1 (1-pound) package confectioners' sugar
2 eggs
Lemon extract (optional)

Combine the cake mix, 1 egg and the butter in a bowl and mix well. Press over the bottom and up the side of a 9×13-inch baking pan. Combine the cream cheese, confectioners' sugar, 2 eggs and the desired amount of lemon extract in a bowl and beat until smooth and creamy. Spoon into the prepared pan. Bake at 350 degrees for 35 to 40 minutes. Cool in the pan on a wire rack or chill, covered, until serving time. Cut into bars.

Seven-Layer Bars

1/2 cup (1 stick) margarine, melted
1 cup graham cracker crumbs
1 (3-ounce) can flaked coconut
1 cup butterscotch chips

1 cup chocolate chips
1 1/2 cups chopped pecans
1 (14-ounce) can sweetened
  condensed milk

Mix the margarine with the graham cracker crumbs in a bowl until evenly moistened. Press over the bottom of a 9×13-inch baking pan. Layer with the coconut, butterscotch chips, chocolate chips and pecans. Pour the sweetened condensed milk evenly over the top. Bake at 350 degrees for 30 to 35 minutes. Cool on a wire rack for 3 to 4 hours. Cut into bars.

Turtle Bars

1 (12-ounce) package vanilla wafers,
  crushed
3/4 cup (1 1/2 sticks) butter, melted

2 cups semisweet chocolate chips
1 cup chopped pecans
1 (12-ounce) jar caramel topping

Mix the vanilla wafer crumbs with the butter in a bowl until evenly moistened. Press over the bottom of a 9×13-inch baking pan. Layer with the chocolate chips and pecans. Drizzle with the caramel topping. Bake at 350 degrees for 12 to 15 minutes. Cool in the pan on a wire rack for 30 minutes. Chill for 30 minutes. Cut into 1 1/2-inch bars and serve.

Crispy Treats

1 cup each corn syrup and sugar
1 cup smooth or chunky peanut butter

1/2 cup baking cocoa
6 cups crisp rice cereal

Combine the corn syrup, sugar, peanut butter and baking cocoa in a 3-quart saucepan and mix well. Cook over low heat, stirring constantly. Bring to a boil, stirring constantly. Remove from the heat and add the cereal, tossing to coat well. Press the mixture into a greased 9×13-inch pan. Cool and cut into 2-inch squares.

Crème de Menthe Brownies

1 cup sugar
1/2 cup (1 stick) butter, softened
4 eggs, beaten
1 cup flour
1/2 teaspoon salt
1 (16-ounce) can chocolate syrup

1 teaspoon vanilla extract
2 cups confectioners' sugar
1/2 cup (1 stick) butter, softened
2 tablespoons green crème de menthe
1 cup semisweet chocolate chips
6 tablespoons (3/4 stick) butter

Cream the sugar and 1/2 cup butter in a bowl until light and fluffy. Add the eggs, flour, salt, chocolate syrup and vanilla and beat until smooth and creamy. Pour into a greased 9×13-inch baking pan. Bake at 350 degrees for 20 to 25 minutes or until brownies pull away from the sides of the pan. Cool completely on a wire rack. Combine the confectioners' sugar, 1/2 cup butter and crème de menthe in a bowl and mix well. Spread evenly over the cooled brownies. Melt the chocolate chips with 6 tablespoons butter in a small saucepan over low heat, stirring frequently. Remove from the heat and let cool until the mixture reaches the desired spreading consistency. Spread over the crème de menthe filling. Chill and cut into small squares to serve.

Chocolate Mint Strips

1 family-size package brownie mix,
    prepared
1/2 (1-pound) package confectioners'
    sugar, sifted (about 2 1/4 cups)
1/4 cup (1/2 stick) butter, softened

1/4 cup milk
4 or 5 drops of oil of peppermint
2 cups semisweet chocolate chips
3 or 4 drops of oil of peppermint
    (optional)

Spread the prepared brownie mix in an 11×17-inch baking pan. Bake at 325 degrees for 18 to 20 minutes or until brownies pull away from the sides of the pan. Cool on a wire rack. Combine the confectioners' sugar, butter, milk and 4 or 5 drops oil of peppermint in a bowl and mix until of the desired spreading consistency. Spread over the cooled brownies; set aside. Melt the chocolate chips in the top of a double boiler over simmering water, stirring frequently. Stir in 3 or 4 drops oil of peppermint for a stronger flavor. Spread evenly over the brownies. Cool completely. Cut into thin strips before refrigerating or freezing.

Chocolate Chip Pan Cookie

1 cup (2 sticks) butter or margarine,
  softened
3/4 cup sugar
3/4 cup packed brown sugar
1 teaspoon vanilla extract
2 eggs

2 1/4 cups flour
1 teaspoon baking soda
1 teaspoon salt
1 cup semisweet chocolate chips
1 cup chopped nuts

Cream the butter, sugar, brown sugar and vanilla in a mixing bowl until light and fluffy. Beat in the eggs. Sift the flour, baking soda and salt together. Add to the creamed mixture gradually, mixing well after each addition. Stir in the chocolate chips and nuts. Spread in a greased 10×15-inch baking pan. Bake at 375 degrees for 20 to 25 minutes or until golden brown. Cool and cut into squares.

Orange Nut Squares

2 cups old-fashioned rolled oats
1 cup flour
3/4 cup packed brown sugar
1 teaspoon cinnamon
1/2 teaspoon baking soda
3/4 cup (1 1/2 sticks) margarine, melted
1 cup raisins

1/2 cup finely chopped walnuts
1/4 cup orange marmalade
1/2 cup confectioners' sugar, sifted
1/4 teaspoon cinnamon
1 tablespoon milk

Combine the oats, flour, brown sugar, 1 teaspoon cinnamon and baking soda in a large bowl and mix well. Stir in the margarine and mix well. Reserve 1 cup of the oat mixture. Press the remaining oat mixture over the bottom of a greased 8×11-inch baking pan. Combine the reserved oat mixture, raisins, walnuts and orange marmalade in a bowl and mix well. Spread evenly over the oat mixture in the pan. Bake at 350 degrees for 25 to 30 minutes or until light brown. Cut into 1-inch squares in the pan while warm. Combine the confectioners' sugar, 1/4 teaspoon cinnamon and milk in a bowl and mix until smooth. Drizzle over the warm squares. Cool completely in the pan. Store in an airtight container.

offee Bars

2 cups flour
1 3/4 cups packed light brown sugar
1 1/2 cups (3 sticks) butter (no
   substitutions)

1 cup chopped pecans
1 cup chocolate chips

Combine the flour and 1 cup of the brown sugar in a bowl. Cut in 1/2 cup of the butter until crumbly. Press over the bottom of a 9×12-inch baking pan. Sprinkle evenly with the pecans. Combine the remaining brown sugar and butter in a saucepan and bring to a boil, stirring constantly. Boil for 1 minute, stirring constantly. Pour over the mixture in the pan.

Bake at 350 degrees for exactly 20 minutes. Let stand for 1 minute. Sprinkle with the chocolate chips and let stand until the chocolate melts. Spread the chocolate evenly. Chill thoroughly. Bring to room temperature before cutting into bars.

utter Cookies

1 cup (2 sticks) butter, softened
1/2 cup sugar
1 egg
1 tablespoon vanilla, lemon or almond
   extract

3 cups sifted flour
1/2 teaspoon baking powder

Cream the butter, sugar and egg in a mixing bowl until light and fluffy. Stir in the vanilla. Sift the flour and baking powder together. Add to the creamed mixture and stir until well mixed. Chill the dough. Roll the dough thinly on a floured surface and cut into desired shapes using cookie cutters. Place on an ungreased cookie sheet.

Bake at 425 degrees for 5 to 7 minutes or until light brown. Cool on the cookie sheet for 1 minute. Remove to a wire rack to cool completely. For a glazed cookie, brush the dough shapes with a mixture of 1 egg yolk and 2 tablespoons water before baking.

Old-Fashioned Tea Cakes

4 eggs
2 1/2 cups sugar
1/2 cup (1 stick) margarine, melted

1/2 cup shortening, melted
2 tablespoons vanilla extract
Self-rising flour

Beat the eggs in a large mixing bowl until thick and pale yellow. Add the sugar, margarine, shortening and vanilla and beat until well blended. Stir in enough flour to make a stiff dough. Roll the dough 1/4 inch thick on a lightly floured surface. Cut with a cookie cutter. Arrange on a nonstick cookie sheet. Bake at 450 degrees until lightly browned. Cool on a wire rack.

Amish Sugar Cookies

1 cup sugar
1 cup confectioners' sugar
1 cup (2 sticks) margarine, softened, or 1
   cup shortening
1 cup vegetable oil
2 eggs

4 1/2 cups flour
1 teaspoon cream of tartar
1 teaspoon baking soda
1 teaspoon salt
1 teaspoon vanilla extract

Beat the sugar, confectioners' sugar, margarine and vegetable oil in a large mixing bowl. Beat in the eggs. Sift the flour, cream of tartar, baking soda and salt together. Add to the sugar mixture with the vanilla and beat until well blended. Drop by heaping teaspoonfuls 2 inches apart onto a greased cookie sheet. Press each cookie with a fork dipped in sugar. Bake at 350 degrees for 10 to 12 minutes or until light brown. Cool on a wire rack.

asy Cookies

1 (2-layer) package chocolate or yellow
   cake mix
1/2 cup vegetable oil

2 eggs
1 cup semisweet chocolate chips
1/2 cup chopped pecans

Combine the cake mix, vegetable oil and eggs in a mixing bowl and beat until smooth. Stir in the chocolate chips and pecans. Drop by heaping teaspoonfuls 2 inches apart onto ungreased cookie sheets. Bake at 350 degrees for 8 to 10 minutes or until light brown. Remove to a wire rack to cool.

White Chocolate Orange Dream Cookies

1 cup (2 sticks) butter or margarine,
   softened
2/3 cup packed light brown sugar
1/2 cup sugar
1 egg
1 tablespoon grated orange zest

2 teaspoons orange extract
2 1/4 cups flour
3/4 teaspoon baking soda
1/2 teaspoon salt
2 cups white chocolate chips

Combine the butter, brown sugar and sugar in a mixing bowl and beat until creamy. Add the egg, orange zest and orange extract and beat until well mixed. Sift the flour, baking soda and salt together. Add to the creamed mixture gradually, beating just until blended after each addition. Stir in the chocolate chips.

Drop by rounded tablespoonfuls 2 inches apart onto an ungreased cookie sheet. Bake at 350 degrees for 10 to 12 minutes or until the edges are lightly browned. Cool on the cookie sheet for 2 minutes. Remove to a wire rack to cool completely.

Chocolate Unbeatables

2 cups confectioners' sugar
1/2 cup self-rising flour
1/4 cup baking cocoa

1/2 cup egg whites (about 3 or 4)
2 cups chopped walnuts
1 cup flaked coconut

Combine the confectioners' sugar, flour, baking cocoa and egg whites in a bowl and mix until well blended. Stir in the walnuts and coconut. Drop by teaspoonfuls onto a greased and floured cookie sheet. Bake at 325 degrees for 10 to 15 minutes or until done. Cool on a wire rack.

Macadamia Chocolate Chip Cookies

3/4 cup (1 1/2 sticks) butter, softened
3/4 cup packed light brown sugar
2/3 cup confectioners' sugar
1 egg
1 teaspoon vanilla extract
2 1/2 cups flour

1 teaspoon salt
1 teaspoon baking soda
2 cups semisweet chocolate chips
1 cup chopped macadamia nuts
1/3 cup chopped pecans

Cream the butter, brown sugar and confectioners' sugar in a mixing bowl until light and fluffy. Add the egg and vanilla and beat until smooth. Sift the flour, salt and baking soda together. Add to the creamed mixture and mix well. Stir in the chocolate chips, macadamia nuts and pecans. Shape the dough into a log. Refrigerate, covered, for 1 hour. Cut into slices and place 2 inches apart on a nonstick cookie sheet. Bake at 325 degrees for 10 minutes. Cool on a wire rack.

Coconut Macadamia Cookies

1/2 cup (1 stick) butter or margarine,
  softened
1/2 cup sugar
1/2 cup packed light brown sugar
1 egg
1 teaspoon vanilla extract

1 1/4 cups flour
1 cup quick-cooking oats
1/2 cup flaked coconut
1/2 teaspoon baking soda
1/4 teaspoon salt
1 cup coarsely chopped macadamia nuts

Combine the butter, sugar, brown sugar, egg and vanilla in a large mixing bowl and beat until fluffy. Combine the flour, oats, coconut, baking soda and salt in a bowl and mix well. Add to the creamed mixture 1/2 at a time, beating at low speed until well mixed. Stir in the macadamia nuts.

Drop by heaping teaspoonfuls 2 inches apart onto a lightly greased cookie sheet. Bake at 350 degrees for 7 to 10 minutes or until the edges are golden brown. Cool on the cookie sheet for 1 minute. Remove to a wire rack to cool completely.

Angel Macaroons

1 (16-ounce) package one-step angel
  food cake mix
1/2 cup water

2 teaspoons almond extract
2 cups flaked coconut

Combine the cake mix, water and almond extract in a bowl. Beat at low speed for 30 seconds, scraping the bowl 1 time. Beat at medium speed for 1 minute. Fold in the coconut. Drop by rounded teaspoonfuls 2 inches apart onto a parchment paper-lined cookie sheet. Bake at 350 degrees for 10 to 12 minutes or until set. Remove the parchment paper with the cookies to a wire rack to cool.

range Blossoms

Juice of 2 lemons
Juice of 4 oranges
2 (1-pound) packages confectioners'
    sugar, sifted

1 (2-layer) package yellow cake mix
1 cup milk
1 teaspoon vanilla extract

Combine the lemon juice, orange juice and confectioners' sugar in a deep wide-mouthed bowl. Beat until smooth and creamy. Set aside. Prepare the cake mix using the package directions, substituting the milk for the water. Stir in the vanilla. Spoon 1 teaspoon batter into each of 48 miniature muffin cups sprayed with baking spray.

Bake at 350 degrees for 10 to 12 minutes or until muffins test done. Invert into the bowl of icing, turning the muffins to coat. Place a sheet of waxed paper underneath a wire cooling rack. Remove the coated muffins with a slotted spoon and place on the wire rack to cool.

ecan Crisps

1 (14-ounce) package cinnamon graham
    crackers
1/2 cup sugar

1 cup (2 sticks) margarine
1 cup finely chopped pecans

Arrange the graham crackers, cinnamon side down, on 2 large nonstick cookie sheets. Combine the sugar, margarine and pecans in a saucepan and bring to a boil, stirring constantly. Boil for 3 minutes, stirring constantly. Drizzle over the crackers with a wooden spoon; do not spread. Bake at 350 degrees for 8 to 10 minutes. Cool completely on the cookie sheet. Break crackers apart to serve.

Butter Pecan Dreams

1 cup (2 sticks) butter, softened
1/2 cup confectioners' sugar
1 teaspoon vanilla extract
2 cups flour

Milk
1 1/2 cups chopped pecans
Confectioners' sugar

Cream the butter and 1/2 cup confectioners' sugar in a bowl until light and fluffy. Stir in the vanilla and flour and mix well. Add a small amount of milk if mixture is too dry. Stir in the pecans. Shape the mixture into small balls and place 2 inches apart on a nonstick cookie sheet. Flatten each ball slightly. Bake at 375 degrees for 20 minutes. Roll the warm cookies in confectioners' sugar.

Wedding Cookies

1 cup (2 sticks) margarine, softened
1/4 cup sugar
2 cups flour

2 teaspoons vanilla extract
1 cup chopped nuts
Confectioners' sugar

Cream the margarine and sugar in a bowl until light and fluffy. Add the flour and vanilla and mix well. Stir in the nuts. Shape the mixture into small balls and place 2 inches apart on a nonstick cookie sheet. Bake at 325 degrees for 12 to 15 minutes or until golden brown. Cool on a wire rack. Roll the cookies in confectioners' sugar to coat.

Pies
&
Desserts

Apple Pie with Crumb Topping

1 (20-ounce) can apple slices
1 unbaked (9-inch) pie shell
1/4 cup self-rising flour
1/2 cup sugar

1 teaspoon cinnamon
1 cup sugar
3/4 cup self-rising flour
1/2 cup (1 stick) butter or margarine

Arrange the apple slices in the bottom of the pie shell. Sift 1/4 cup flour, 1/2 cup sugar and cinnamon together. Sprinkle evenly over the apple slices. Combine 1 cup sugar and 3/4 cup flour in a bowl and mix well. Cut in the butter using a pastry blender until crumbly. Sprinkle the mixture over the top of the pie. Bake at 325 degrees for 1 hour or until bubbly and golden brown. You may use a food processor to prepare the crumb topping if desired.

Blueberry Cream Pie

1/2 cup chopped pecans
2 unbaked (9-inch) pie shells
1 (1-pound) package confectioners' sugar

8 ounces cream cheese, softened
16 ounces whipped topping
1 (21-ounce) can blueberry pie filling

Sprinkle equal portions of the pecans in each pie shell and press lightly. Bake pie shells using package directions. Let stand until cool. Combine the confectioners' sugar and cream cheese in a food processor and pulse until well mixed. Remove to a mixing bowl and fold in the whipped topping. Pour into the baked crusts and top with the pie filling.

hocolate Chess Pie

1 cup sugar
3 eggs, beaten
3 tablespoons cornmeal
3 tablespoons baking cocoa
1/2 cup (1 stick) butter or margarine,
    melted

1/2 cup light corn syrup
1 teaspoon vanilla extract
1 unbaked (9-inch) pie shell

Beat the sugar and eggs together in a large bowl. Add the cornmeal, baking cocoa, butter, corn syrup and vanilla and mix well. Pour into the pie shell. Bake at 325 degrees for 45 minutes or until the filling is set. Chill before slicing and serving.

rench Silk Pie

2 ounces unsweetened chocolate
1/2 cup (1 stick) butter or margarine,
    softened
3/4 cup sugar
2 eggs, or equivalent amount of
    pasteurized egg substitute

4 ounces whipped topping
    (about 13/4 cups)
1 baked (9-inch) pie shell
3/4 cup whipping cream
2 tablespoons confectioners' sugar
Chocolate shavings (optional)

Place the unsweetened chocolate in the top of a double boiler over water. Bring the water to a boil. Reduce the heat to low and cook until the chocolate melts, stirring constantly. Remove from the heat and set aside to cool.

Cream the butter in a bowl. Add the sugar gradually, beating at medium speed of an electric mixer until light and fluffy. Stir in the cooled chocolate. Add the eggs 1 at a time, beating for 5 minutes after each addition. Fold in the whipped topping and spoon into the pie shell. Chill for 2 hours.

Beat the whipping cream in a bowl until foamy. Add the confectioners' sugar gradually, beating until soft peaks form. Spread evenly over the chilled pie. Garnish with chocolate shavings.

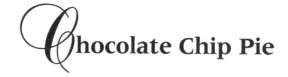

Chocolate Chip Pie

4 eggs
1 cup (2 sticks) butter, melted
2 teaspoons vanilla extract
2 cups chopped nuts

2 cups sugar
1 cup flour
1 1/2 cups chocolate chips
2 unbaked (9-inch) pie shells

Beat the eggs in a large bowl until thick and pale yellow. Add the butter, vanilla and nuts and mix well. Add the sugar, flour and chocolate chips and mix well. Pour into the pie shells. Bake at 350 degrees for 40 to 60 minutes or until set. Serve warm with vanilla ice cream and a drizzle of caramel sauce over the top.

German Sweet Chocolate Pie

1 1/2 cups sugar
3 tablespoons baking cocoa
1/2 cup (1 stick) butter, melted
1/3 cup milk
2 eggs

1 tablespoon vanilla extract
1/2 cup flaked coconut
1/2 cup chopped pecans
1 unbaked (9-inch) pie shell

Combine the sugar, baking cocoa, butter, milk, eggs and vanilla in a large bowl and beat until well blended. Stir in the coconut and pecans. Pour into the pie shell. Bake at 325 degrees for 1 hour or until set. Cool before slicing.

aramel Coconut Pie

1/4 cup (1/2 stick) butter or margarine
1 (7-ounce) package flaked coconut
1/2 cup chopped pecans
8 ounces cream cheese, softened
1 (14-ounce) can sweetened
    condensed milk

16 ounces whipped topping
2 baked (9-inch) deep-dish pie shells
1 (12-ounce) jar caramel topping

Melt the butter in a large skillet over medium heat. Add the coconut and pecans and cook until golden, stirring frequently. Cool slightly. Beat the cream cheese with the sweetened condensed milk in a bowl at medium speed until smooth. Fold in the whipped topping. Spread 1/4 of the cream cheese mixture in the bottom of each pie shell and drizzle each with 1/4 of the caramel topping. Sprinkle 1/4 of the coconut mixture over the top of each pie. Repeat the layers once using the remaining cream cheese mixture, caramel topping and coconut mixture. Freeze, covered, for 8 hours or longer. Let stand at room temperature for 10 to 15 minutes before serving.

rench Coconut Pie

3 eggs
1 cup sugar
1/4 cup buttermilk
1 teaspoon vanilla extract

1/2 cup (1 stick) butter, melted
1 1/2 cups flaked coconut
1 unbaked (9-inch) pie shell

Beat the eggs in a medium bowl until thick and pale yellow. Add the sugar, buttermilk, vanilla and butter and beat until well mixed. Stir in the coconut and pour into the pie shell. Bake at 375 degrees for 10 minutes. Reduce the oven temperature to 300 degrees and continue baking until the filling is set and the top is golden brown.

oconut Cream Pie

2/3 cup sugar	2 tablespoons margarine
1/2 cup flour	2 teaspoons vanilla extract
1/4 teaspoon salt	1 baked (9-inch) pie shell
2 cups milk	3 egg whites, at room temperature
3 egg yolks, lightly beaten	1/4 teaspoon cream of tartar
1 1/3 cups flaked coconut	6 tablespoons sugar

Combine 2/3 cup sugar, flour and salt in a saucepan. Stir in the milk gradually. Cook over medium heat until bubbly, stirring constantly. Stir a small amount of the hot mixture into the egg yolks. Pour the egg yolk mixture into the hot mixture immediately. Cook for 2 minutes, stirring constantly. Add 1 cup of the coconut, margarine and vanilla and mix well. Pour into the pie shell.

Combine the egg whites and cream of tartar in a bowl and beat until foamy. Add 6 tablespoons sugar gradually, beating until soft peaks form. Spread the meringue evenly over the pie, sealing to the edge. Sprinkle with the remaining coconut. Bake at 400 degrees for 8 minutes or until meringue peaks are golden brown.

gg Custard Pie

1/2 cup (1 stick) butter or margarine, softened	2 1/2 cups milk
	1 teaspoon vanilla extract
1 1/2 cups sugar	1/2 teaspoon nutmeg
1/4 cup cornstarch	Pinch of salt
4 eggs	2 unbaked (9-inch) pie shells

Cream the butter and sugar in a bowl until light and fluffy. Add the cornstarch and mix well. Beat in the eggs 1 at a time. Add the milk, vanilla, nutmeg and salt and beat until well blended. Pour into the pie shells. Bake at 400 degrees for 15 minutes. Reduce the oven temperature to 325 degrees. Bake for 20 minutes longer or until the custard is set.

emon Chess Pie

4 eggs
1 1/2 cups sugar
1/3 cup milk
3 tablespoons cornmeal

1/2 cup (1 stick) margarine, softened
1 tablespoon lemon extract
1 unbaked (9-inch) pie shell

Beat the eggs with the sugar in a bowl until blended. Add the milk, cornmeal, margarine and lemon extract and beat until well blended. Pour into the pie shell. Bake at 325 degrees for 30 to 35 minutes or until the filling is set in the center.

ℒemon Meringue Pie

1 (14-ounce) can sweetened condensed
   milk
1/3 cup lemon juice
1/2 teaspoon lemon extract
3 egg yolks

1 (8-inch) graham cracker pie shell
3 egg whites
1/4 teaspoon cream of tartar
1/4 cup sugar

Combine the sweetened condensed milk, lemon juice and lemon extract in a bowl and mix well. Blend in the egg yolks. Pour into the pie shell. Beat the egg whites with the cream of tartar in a mixer bowl until soft peaks form. Add the sugar gradually, beating until stiff peaks form. Spread the meringue evenly over the pie filling, sealing to the edge. Bake at 325 degrees for 12 to 15 minutes or until the meringue is golden brown.

Pecan Pie

1/2 cup (1 stick) butter, melted
1 cup sugar
1 cup light corn syrup
4 eggs, beaten

1 teaspoon vanilla extract
1/4 teaspoon salt
1 unbaked (9-inch) pie shell
1 cup chopped pecans

Combine the butter, sugar and corn syrup in a saucepan and mix well. Cook over low heat until the sugar is dissolved, stirring constantly. Remove from the heat and cool. Add the eggs, vanilla and salt and mix until well blended. Pour into the pie shell and top with the pecans. Bake at 325 degrees for 50 to 55 minutes or until set.

Variation: For a Rum Pecan Pie, prepare as directed above, adding 3 tablespoons rum with the eggs.

Pecan Cream Cheese Pie

8 ounces cream cheese, softened
1 egg
1/4 cup sugar
2 teaspoons vanilla extract
3/4 cup light corn syrup

3 eggs
2 tablespoons sugar
1 unbaked deep-dish pie shell
1/2 cup chopped pecans

Beat the cream cheese, 1 egg, 1/4 cup sugar and half the vanilla together in a bowl until smooth. Beat the corn syrup, remaining vanilla, 3 eggs and 2 tablespoons sugar together in a bowl until smooth. Spoon the cream cheese mixture into the pie shell. Sprinkle evenly with the pecans and top with the corn syrup mixture. Bake at 375 degrees for 35 minutes.

trawberry Pie

1 quart fresh strawberries, rinsed, drained
1 cup water
1 cup sugar
2 tablespoons cornstarch
Few drops of red food coloring

1 (3-ounce) package strawberry gelatin
1 baked (9-inch) pie shell
1 container whipped topping, or 1 cup
  whipped cream

Hull the strawberries and cut into halves if large. Combine the water, sugar and cornstarch in a small saucepan and mix well. Cook over low heat until the mixture is thick and clear, stirring constantly. Add the food coloring and 1/4 cup of the strawberry gelatin and stir to dissolve. Set aside to cool.

Reserve any remaining gelatin for another use or discard. Arrange the strawberries in the bottom of the pie shell. Pour the cornstarch mixture over the top. Refrigerate until ready to serve. Top with the whipped topping just before serving.

weet Potato Pie

2 large sweet potatoes, cooked, peeled, or
  1 (17-ounce) can sweet potatoes,
  drained
1 1/2 cups sugar
1/2 cup milk
1/2 cup (1 stick) butter or margarine,
  melted

3 eggs
1 teaspoon vanilla extract
1 teaspoon orange extract
1/4 teaspoon salt
1 unbaked (9-inch) pie shell

Place the sweet potatoes in a mixing bowl and beat at medium speed until smooth. Add the sugar, milk, butter, eggs, vanilla, orange extract and salt and beat until well blended. Pour into the pie shell and smooth with a spatula. Bake at 350 degrees for 45 to 50 minutes or until a knife inserted in the center comes out clean.

Vanilla Cream Pie

3/4 cup sugar
1/4 cup plus 2 teaspoons cornstarch
1/8 teaspoon salt
3 egg yolks, beaten
3 cups milk

41/2 teaspoons butter or margarine
11/2 teaspoons vanilla extract
1 baked (9-inch) pie shell
3/4 cup whipping cream
1/3 cup sifted confectioners' sugar

Combine the sugar, cornstarch and salt in a heavy saucepan and mix well. Blend the egg yolks and milk in a bowl and add to the cornstarch mixture gradually, mixing well. Cook over medium heat until the mixture thickens and boils, stirring constantly. Boil for 1 minute, stirring constantly. Remove from the heat and stir in the butter and vanilla. Pour into the pie shell immediately. Cover the filling with waxed paper and let stand for 30 minutes. Chill until firm. Beat the whipping cream in a bowl until foamy. Add the confectioners' sugar gradually, beating until soft peaks form. Spread the whipped cream over the filling. Chill until serving time.

Cherry Tarts

3 ounces cream cheese, softened
1/2 cup (1 stick) margarine, softened
1 cup flour
1/4 cup ground nuts
8 ounces cream cheese, softened

1 (14-ounce) can sweetened condensed milk
1/3 cup lemon juice
1 (21-ounce) can cherry pie filling

Cream 3 ounces cream cheese with the margarine in a bowl until smooth. Add the flour and nuts and mix well; chill. Press small pieces of the dough over the bottoms and sides of miniature tart pans. Bake at 300 degrees for 25 minutes.

Combine 8 ounces cream cheese, sweetened condensed milk and lemon juice in a bowl and beat until well mixed. Spoon into the baked tart shells. Top each with 1 cherry from the pie filling. Filling makes enough for 2 recipes of the tart shells.

ecan Tassies

1 cup flour
3 ounces cream cheese, softened
7 tablespoons butter, softened
3/4 cup packed light brown sugar
3/4 cup chopped pecans
1 egg

1 tablespoon butter or margarine,
  softened
1 teaspoon vanilla extract
Dash of salt
Confectioners' sugar (optional)

Combine the flour, cream cheese and 7 tablespoons butter in a bowl and beat until well mixed. Divide and shape the dough into 24 equal balls; chill. Press 1 dough ball over the bottom and side of each of 24 greased 1 3/4-inch tart pans. Place the tart pans on a baking sheet and set aside.

Combine the brown sugar, pecans, egg, 1 tablespoon butter, vanilla and salt in a bowl and mix well. Fill the tart shells 3/4 full. Bake at 350 degrees for 20 minutes or until browned. Dust with confectioners' sugar before serving.

hocolate Pecan Tartlets

36 frozen miniature phyllo shells
1/3 cup semisweet chocolate chips
1 cup finely chopped pecans, toasted
3/4 cup packed light brown sugar

1 tablespoon butter or margarine,
  softened
1/4 cup bourbon
1 egg, lightly beaten

Arrange the phyllo shells on a lightly greased 10×15-inch baking pan. Sprinkle the chocolate chips into the shells. Combine the pecans, brown sugar, butter, bourbon and egg in a bowl and mix well. Spoon over the chocolate chips in the shells. Bake at 350 degrees for 20 minutes or until golden brown. Store in an airtight container for up to 3 days or freeze for up to 1 month.

 ittle Fried Pies

3 cups flour	4 cups dried apples or peaches
1 teaspoon salt	2 cups water
3/4 cup shortening	1/2 cup sugar
1 egg, beaten	1/2 teaspoon cinnamon
1/4 cup water	Vegetable oil for frying
1 teaspoon vinegar	

Combine the flour and salt in a bowl. Cut in the shortening with a pastry blender until the mixture resembles coarse meal. Blend the egg and water in a small bowl. Sprinkle over the flour mixture. Add the vinegar and stir gently with a fork until the mixture forms a dough. Shape into a ball and wrap in waxed paper. Chill for 1 hour or longer.

Combine the apples and water in a large saucepan and bring the mixture to a boil. Reduce the heat and simmer, covered, for 30 minutes or until the apples are tender, stirring occasionally. Cool. Mash slightly if necessary. Stir in the sugar and cinnamon and set aside.

Divide the dough into thirds. Roll each portion 1/4 inch thick on waxed paper and cut into four 5-inch circles. Place 2 tablespoons of the apple mixture on one half of each dough circle. Moisten the edge of each circle with fingers dipped in water. Fold the circles in half and seal the edges, pressing firmly with a fork dipped in flour.

Pour 1/2 inch vegetable oil into a large skillet. Heat the oil to 375 degrees. Fry the pies in the hot oil until golden brown on both sides, turning once. Remove and drain on paper towels. Sprinkle with additional sugar.

anana Split Dessert

2 cups graham cracker crumbs
1/2 cup (1 stick) margarine, melted
3 eggs, or equivalent egg substitute
11/2 cups (3 sticks) margarine, softened
1 cup confectioners' sugar

3 to 4 bananas, sliced
1 (20-ounce) can crushed pineapple, drained
16 ounces whipped topping

Combine the graham cracker crumbs and 1/2 cup melted margarine in a bowl and mix until evenly moistened. Press over the bottom of a 9×13-inch dish. Combine the eggs, 11/2 cups softened margarine and confectioners' sugar in a bowl and beat for 15 minutes. Pour into the crust. Layer with the banana slices and crushed pineapple. Spread with the whipped topping. Garnish with chopped nuts and cherries. Refrigerate overnight before serving.

lueberry Nut Crunch

1 (20-ounce) can crushed pineapple
3 cups blueberries
3/4 cup sugar

1 (2-layer) package yellow cake mix
1 cup chopped pecans
1/2 cup (1 stick) butter, thinly sliced

Spread the undrained pineapple in a 9×13-inch baking pan. Scatter the blueberries over the pineapple. Layer evenly with the sugar, cake mix and pecans. Cover the pecans with the butter slices. Bake at 350 degrees for 35 to 40 minutes or until brown.

Cheesecake

1³/4 cups fine graham cracker crumbs
1/2 cup (1 stick) butter or margarine, melted
2 tablespoons sugar
24 ounces cream cheese, softened

4 eggs
1 cup sugar
2 teaspoons vanilla extract
2 cups sour cream
2 tablespoons sugar

For the crust, combine the graham cracker crumbs, butter and 2 tablespoons sugar in a bowl and mix well. Press over the bottom and halfway up the side of a springform pan.

For the filling, beat the cream cheese in a bowl until smooth. Add the eggs, 1 cup sugar and vanilla and mix well. Pour into the pan. Bake at 350 degrees for 40 minutes. Remove the cheesecake and increase the oven temperature to 450 degrees.

For the topping, beat the sour cream with 2 tablespoons sugar in a bowl for 5 minutes. Pour over the cheesecake and bake for 7 minutes longer.

Company Cheesecake

1³/4 cups fine graham cracker crumbs
1/4 cup finely chopped walnuts
1/2 teaspoon cinnamon
1/2 cup (1 stick) butter, melted
3 eggs, beaten
16 ounces cream cheese, softened

1 cup sugar
1/4 teaspoon salt
2 teaspoons vanilla extract
1/4 teaspoon almond extract
3 cups sour cream

Combine the graham cracker crumbs, walnuts, cinnamon and butter in a bowl and mix well. Press over the bottom and 2/3 up the side of a 9-inch springform pan. Combine the eggs, cream cheese, sugar, salt, vanilla and almond extract in a bowl and beat until smooth. Blend in the sour cream. Pour into the prepared pan.

Bake at 375 degrees for 35 minutes or just until set. Cool on a wire rack. Chill for 4 to 5 hours. Place on a serving plate and loosen the cheesecake from the side of the pan. Remove the side of the pan to serve. Filling will be soft.

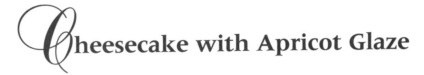

Cheesecake with Apricot Glaze

2 cups graham cracker crumbs
1/4 cup sugar
1/2 cup (1 stick) butter or margarine,
   melted
7 eggs
32 ounces cream cheese, softened
1 3/4 cups sugar
2 teaspoons vanilla extract

2 cups sour cream
1/2 cup sugar
1/8 teaspoon vanilla extract
1 (10-ounce) jar apricot jam
1/4 cup sugar
1/4 cup water
1 tablespoon rum or brandy

Combine the graham cracker crumbs, 1/4 cup sugar and butter in a bowl and mix well. Press over the bottom and 1 inch up the side of a 10-inch springform pan. Chill for 1 hour. Beat the eggs in a bowl at medium speed. Add the cream cheese and beat until well blended. Add 1 3/4 cups sugar gradually, beating until well mixed. Stir in 2 teaspoons vanilla. Pour into the chilled crust.

Bake at 350 degrees for 1 1/4 hours. Cool on a wire rack for 10 minutes. Increase the oven temperature to 425 degrees. Combine the sour cream, 1/2 cup sugar and 1/8 teaspoon vanilla in a bowl and mix well. Spread over the cheesecake. Bake at 425 degrees for 5 to 7 minutes or until set. Cool on a wire rack for 1 hour. Chill, covered, for 10 hours or longer.

Combine the apricot jam, 1/4 cup sugar and water in a small saucepan and mix well. Cook over low heat until the mixture is the consistency of syrup, stirring occasionally. Remove from the heat and stir in the rum; strain. Cool. Place the cheesecake on a serving plate. Loosen the cheesecake from the side of the pan. Remove the side of the pan. Drizzle the apricot glaze over slices of cheesecake to serve. Garnish with strawberry halves.

Variation: For a Cherry Glaze, substitute cherry preserves for the apricot jam; do not strain before serving.

raline Cheesecake

1¹/2 cups graham cracker crumbs
¹/2 cup (1 stick) butter, melted
¹/2 cup sugar
1 teaspoon cinnamon
32 ounces cream cheese, softened

3 eggs
1 teaspoon vanilla extract
2 cups packed brown sugar
1 cup chopped pecans
3 tablespoons flour

Combine the graham cracker crumbs, butter, sugar and cinnamon in a bowl and mix well. Press over the bottom and up the side of a 9-inch springform pan. Cream the cream cheese in a large bowl until smooth. Add the eggs and vanilla and beat until fluffy. Add the brown sugar, pecans and flour and stir just until combined. Spoon into the crust. Bake at 350 degrees for 1 hour and 10 minutes. Cool on a wire rack. Chill until serving time. Place on a serving plate. Loosen the cheesecake from the side of the pan. Remove the side of the pan and serve.

hocolate Torte

1¹/2 cups flour
³/4 cup (1¹/2 sticks) butter, softened
1 cup chopped nuts
8 ounces cream cheese, softened
1¹/4 cups confectioners' sugar
1 small container whipped topping

2 (4-ounce) packages chocolate or
　butterscotch instant pudding mix
3 cups milk
1 large container whipped topping
1 cup chopped pecans, toasted

Combine the flour, butter and 1 cup nuts in a bowl and mix well. Spread in a 9×13-inch baking pan. Bake at 350 degrees for 20 minutes; cool. Combine the cream cheese, confectioners' sugar and small container of whipped topping in a bowl and mix well. Spoon over the cooled crust.

Beat the pudding mix with the milk in a bowl until well combined. Pour over the cream cheese mixture in the pan. Let stand until set. Spread with large container of whipped topping and sprinkle with 1 cup pecans.

Chocolate Éclair Dessert

1 (16-ounce) package graham crackers
1 (6-ounce) package vanilla instant
    pudding mix
2 1/2 cups milk
12 ounces whipped topping

1/3 cup baking cocoa
1/2 cup (1 stick) margarine
1 cup sugar
1 teaspoon vanilla extract
1/4 cup evaporated milk

Line a 9×13-inch pan with a few of the graham crackers. Prepare the pudding mix using 2 1/2 cups milk. Fold in the whipped topping. Spread over the graham crackers. Top with a layer of graham crackers. Combine the baking cocoa, margarine, sugar, vanilla and evaporated milk in a saucepan and bring to a boil, stirring constantly. Boil for 1 minute, stirring constantly; do not boil longer. Remove from the heat and whisk the mixture briefly. Pour over the graham crackers in the pan. Refrigerate, covered, overnight. Reserve any remaining graham crackers for another use.

Orange Cream Fruit Dip

8 ounces cream cheese, softened
1 (7-ounce) jar marshmallow creme
2 tablespoons fresh orange juice

1/2 teaspoon orange extract
Fresh whole strawberries

Combine the cream cheese, marshmallow creme, orange juice and orange extract in a food processor. Process until smooth and creamy. Remove to a serving bowl and chill, covered, until serving time. Serve with the strawberries for dipping.
Variation: Substitute 1 to 2 tablespoons Grand Marnier for the orange extract.

Strawberry Dip

1 (7-ounce) jar marshmallow creme
8 ounces cream cheese, softened

Fresh whole strawberries, rinsed, drained

Combine the marshmallow creme and cream cheese in a bowl and whip until well blended. Spoon into a serving bowl and serve with the strawberries for dipping.

Yogurt Sour Cream Dip

1 cup yogurt
1 cup sour cream
2 tablespoons honey

3/4 teaspoon ginger
1/2 teaspoon lemon juice
Sliced fresh fruit

Combine the yogurt, sour cream, honey, ginger and lemon juice in a bowl and whisk until well blended. Spoon into a serving bowl and refrigerate, covered, for 1 hour before serving. Serve with sliced fresh fruit for dipping.

Homemade Ice Cream

2 1/2 cups sugar
4 eggs
1 (12-ounce) can Carnation
   evaporated milk
1 tablespoon vanilla extract

1 (14-ounce) can sweetened
   condensed milk
1/8 teaspoon salt
Milk

Beat the sugar with the eggs and evaporated milk in a bowl until smooth. Add the vanilla, sweetened condensed milk and salt and mix well. Pour into a 4-quart or 1-gallon ice cream freezer container. Add milk to the fill line. Freeze using the manufacturer's directions. Let ripen for 1 hour or longer before serving.

Chocolate Ice Cream

3 eggs
1 cup sugar
4 cups half-and-half
2 cups heavy cream

1 cup chocolate syrup
1 tablespoon vanilla extract
3 cups (about) milk

Beat the eggs in a bowl at medium speed until frothy. Add the sugar gradually, beating until thick. Add the half-and-half, heavy cream, chocolate syrup and vanilla and mix well. Pour into a large heavy saucepan. Cook over medium heat until the mixture comes to a boil, stirring constantly. Boil for 1 minute, stirring constantly. Allow mixture to cool.

Pour into the freezer container of a 1-gallon hand-turned or electric ice cream freezer. Add enough of the milk to fill the container 3/4 full. Freeze using the manufacturer's directions. Let ripen for 1 hour or longer before serving.

Caramel Vanilla Ice Cream

2 (14-ounce) cans sweetened
  condensed milk
4 eggs
2 cups sugar

4 cups half-and-half
2 cups heavy cream
4 cups milk

Pour the sweetened condensed milk into two 8-inch pie plates and cover each with aluminum foil. Place each pie plate in a larger shallow pan filled with hot water to a depth of 1/4 inch. Bake at 425 degrees for 1 hour and 20 minutes or until the sweetened condensed milk is thick and caramel colored, adding hot water to the larger pans as necessary. Set aside to cool.

Beat the eggs in a large bowl at medium speed until thick and pale yellow. Add the sugar gradually, beating until light and fluffy. Add the caramelized milk, half-and-half and heavy cream, beating constantly until well blended. Pour into the freezer container of a 1 1/2-gallon hand-turned or electric ice cream freezer. Add the milk and stir until well mixed. Freeze using the manufacturer's directions. Let ripen for 1 hour or longer before serving.

eorgia Peach Cobbler

8 cups sliced peaches
2 cups sugar
3 tablespoons flour
$1/2$ teaspoon nutmeg
1 teaspoon vanilla extract

$1/3$ cup butter, softened
$1/3$ cup boiling water
$2/3$ cup butter, softened
2 cups flour
$1 1/2$ teaspoons salt

Combine the peaches, sugar, 3 tablespoons flour and nutmeg in a Dutch oven. Set aside to allow a syrup to form. Bring the mixture to a boil, stirring constantly. Reduce the heat to low and simmer for 10 minutes or until the peaches are tender. Remove from the heat and stir in the vanilla and $1/3$ cup butter. Spoon half the mixture into a baking dish.

Combine the boiling water and $2/3$ cup butter in a bowl and stir until the butter is melted. Add 2 cups flour and salt and stir to make a dough. Divide the dough in half. Roll one half out on a floured surface to fit the shape of the baking dish. Place the dough over the peach mixture in the pan.

Bake at 475 degrees for 12 minutes. Spoon the remaining peach mixture over the baked pastry. Roll the remaining dough out on a floured surface and cut into strips. Arrange lattice-fashion over the top. Bake for 15 to 20 minutes longer or until browned.

ruit Pizza

1 recipe sugar cookie dough, 1 package
  sugar cookie mix, or 1 tube refrigerated
  sugar cookie dough
8 ounces cream cheese, softened
1 (7-ounce) jar marshmallow creme
Almond, lemon or vanilla extract to taste
10 or 11 peach slices
Fruit-Fresh
1 (11-ounce) can mandarin oranges,
  drained

1 (8-ounce) can crushed pineapple,
  drained
2 kiwifruit, sliced
12 strawberries
Fresh or frozen blueberries
1 cup apple juice
4 teaspoons arrowroot

Spray a disposable pizza pan with nonstick cooking spray. Line the pan with the prepared sugar cookie dough, spreading evenly to the edge. Bake at 350 degrees for 10 to 12 minutes or just until light golden brown. Combine the cream cheese, marshmallow creme and the desired amount of extract in a bowl and mix well. Spread evenly over the baked layer. Dip the peach slices in the Fruit-Fresh.

Arrange the peaches, mandarin oranges, pineapple, kiwifruit, strawberries and blueberries over the cream cheese mixture in the desired design, beginning at the outer edge and working toward the center. Combine the apple juice and arrowroot in a small saucepan and mix well. Cook over medium-high heat until thickened, stirring constantly; do not boil. Remove from the heat; cool. Brush the glaze evenly over the fruit pizza using a pastry brush.

Easy Banana Pudding

3 (4-ounce) packages vanilla instant
  pudding mix
5 cups milk
1 cup sour cream

12 ounces whipped topping
1 (16-ounce) package vanilla wafers
6 bananas, sliced

Combine the pudding mix and milk in a large bowl and mix well. Add the sour cream and half the whipped topping and mix well. Layer the vanilla wafers, bananas and pudding mixture 1/3 at a time in a large dish. Top with the remaining whipped topping. Chill until serving time.

Banana Pudding

3/4 cup sugar
3 tablespoons flour
2 cups milk
3 egg yolks
1 teaspoon vanilla extract
1/4 cup (1/2 stick) butter

3 medium bananas, sliced
Vanilla wafers
3 egg whites
1/4 teaspoon cream of tartar
6 tablespoons sugar

Combine 3/4 cup sugar and flour in the top of a double boiler and mix well. Add the milk gradually, stirring to blend. Cook over simmering water until the mixture thickens, stirring constantly. Beat the egg yolks lightly in a small bowl. Add a small amount of the hot custard to the egg yolks and stir quickly. Add the egg yolk mixture to the hot custard and cook for 2 minutes longer, stirring constantly. Remove from the heat and stir in the vanilla and butter. Let cool.

Reserve 3/4 cup of the custard. Layer the remaining custard, bananas and vanilla wafers 1/3 at a time in a 9×13-inch baking dish. Spread the reserved custard over the top. Beat the egg whites with the cream of tartar and 6 tablespoons sugar in a bowl until stiff peaks form. Spread the meringue over the pudding, sealing to the edges. Bake at 350 degrees until the meringue is golden brown.

unch Bowl Dessert

1 (2-layer) package yellow cake mix
2 (10-ounce) packages frozen
    strawberries, thawed
1/4 cup sugar
2 tablespoons cornstarch
1 tablespoon lemon juice
1 (6-ounce) package vanilla instant
    pudding mix

3 cups milk
1 (14-ounce) can sweetened condensed
    milk
18 ounces whipped topping
1 (13-ounce) can sliced peaches
4 bananas, or 1 can flaked coconut

Prepare and bake the cake mix using the package directions for a 9x13-inch cake pan. Let stand until cool.

Drain the strawberries, reserving the liquid. Place the reserved liquid in a 2-cup measuring bowl. Add enough water to measure 1 1/2 cups. Combine the liquid, sugar and cornstarch in a saucepan. Cook over medium heat until thickened, stirring constantly. Remove from heat. Stir in the lemon juice and strawberries. Let stand until cool.

Prepare the pudding mix in a large bowl according to package directions, using 3 cups milk. Add the condensed milk and half the whipped topping and mix well.

Tear the cake into small pieces. Layer the cake, strawberry mixture, pudding mixture, peaches and bananas one-third at a time in a punch bowl or large glass bowl. Spread with the remaining whipped topping. Chill until serving time. Garnish with pecans or walnuts and maraschino cherries.

utterscotch Sauce

2 cups packed brown sugar
3/4 cup plus 2 tablespoons light
  corn syrup

1/4 cup (1/2 stick) butter or margarine
1/8 teaspoon salt
1 (5-ounce) can evaporated milk

Combine the brown sugar, corn syrup and butter in a saucepan. Bring the mixture to a boil over medium heat, stirring constantly. Remove from the heat and stir in the salt and evaporated milk. Serve the warm sauce over ice cream. For microwave preparation, combine the brown sugar, corn syrup and butter in a 1-quart glass measuring cup. Microwave on High for 3 to 4 minutes, stirring once. Stir in the salt and evaporated milk.

reamy Caramel Sauce

1 cup sugar
1/2 cup (1 stick) butter, softened

1/2 cup half-and-half

Sprinkle the sugar in a large cast-iron skillet. Cook over medium heat until the sugar is melted and light brown, stirring constantly with a wooden spoon. Remove from the heat and add the butter, stirring until well blended. Return the mixture to low heat and add the half-and-half 1 tablespoon at a time, stirring constantly. Cook over low heat for 10 minutes or until the mixture is thickened and creamy, stirring constantly. Serve the warm sauce over ice cream or pound cake.

$\mathscr{H}$ot Fudge Sauce

1 cup sugar
1 cup light corn syrup
1/2 cup baking cocoa

1/2 cup evaporated milk
1/4 cup (1/2 stick) margarine, softened
1 teaspoon vanilla extract

Combine the sugar, corn syrup, baking cocoa, evaporated milk and margarine in a heavy 2-quart saucepan and mix well. Bring the mixture to a boil over medium heat, stirring constantly. Boil for 3 minutes, stirring occasionally. Remove from the heat and stir in the vanilla. Serve over ice cream or cake. Refrigerate leftovers in a tightly covered container.

$\mathscr{P}$raline Sauce

1 1/2 cups chopped pecans
1/4 cup (1/2 stick) butter or margarine
1 1/4 cups packed light brown sugar

3/4 cup light corn syrup
3 tablespoons flour
1 (5-ounce) can evaporated milk

Spread the pecans on a baking sheet. Bake at 300 degrees for 15 minutes; set aside. Melt the butter in a medium saucepan. Add the brown sugar, corn syrup and flour and mix well. Bring the mixture to a boil, stirring constantly. Reduce the heat and simmer for 5 minutes, stirring constantly. Remove from the heat and cool to lukewarm. Stir in the evaporated milk and toasted pecans gradually. Serve the warm sauce over ice cream.

For microwave preparation, spread the pecans on a large glass pizza plate. Microwave on High for 5 to 6 minutes or until lightly toasted, stirring every 2 minutes. Place the butter in a 1-quart glass bowl. Microwave on High for 55 seconds or until melted. Add the brown sugar, corn syrup and flour and mix well. Microwave on High for 3 to 4 minutes or until the mixture is very hot, stirring every 2 minutes. Stir in the evaporated milk and pecans gradually.

Index

Mother's Finest
Southern Cooking Made Easy

Mother's Finest Catering
P.O. Box 1765
Mableton, Georgia 30126
Phone: (770) 944-9277
Fax: (770) 944-6500
Website: www.mothersfinestcatering.com

Please send _____ copies of *Southern Cooking Made Easy* at $19.95 each $ _____

Georgia residents add sales tax at $1.23 each $ _____

Add shipping and handling at $3.50 each $ _____

Total $ _____

_____
Name

_____
Street Address

_____
City   State   Zip

_____
Telephone

Method of Payment: [   ] American Express   [   ] Discover
                     [   ] MasterCard   [   ] VISA
                     [   ] Check payable to Mother's Finest Cookbook

_____
Account Number   Expiration Date

_____
Cardholder Name

_____
Signature

Photocopies will be accepted.